HOW TO ANALYZE PEOPLE

The Guide to Speed Reading People, Analyzing Body Language, Through Behavioral Psychology, Understand What Every Person is Saying Using Emotional Intelligence and Dark Psychology

engaging in the rendering of legal, financial, medical or professional advice. The content within this book has been derived from various sources. Please consult a licensed professional before attempting any techniques outlined in this book.

By reading this document, the reader agrees that under no circumstances is the author responsible for any losses, direct or indirect, which are incurred as a result of the use of information contained within this document, including, but not limited to, — errors, omissions, or inaccuracies.

TABLE OF CONTENTS

INTRODUCTION

Much of basic common body language is the same all over the world despite religion and racial differences. Some examples of this are smiling when you're happy or scowling when you are sad or angry. The nodding of the head is almost completely universally used to indicate an affirmation of sorts. It is believed that this form of affirmation is a genetic predisposition because individuals who were born blind still use this form of body language even though they never learned to use it visually.

This then brings me to an interesting point about body language and whether it is a learned action or genetic action. This is a debate that is ongoing and is still being researched even up to this day. Some forms of body language can be traced back to animal ancestry and are believed to be purely genetic. This is the action of sneering at another person in anger or irritation. An animal's a similar action to this is done when preparing for an attack.

There are three basic rules for an accurate reading of

somebody's body language. You must keep these three rules in mind when attempting to analyze any person for their body language.

1. Reading Clusters of Gestures Rather Than an Individual

You should never try to analyze or interpret a single solitary gesture separately from all of the others. You have to look at the entire picture. This means that you have to look at every action of the person's body and compare it to the rest of them. It is easy to remember this rule when you think of body language as just that: a language. As with any vocally spoken language, body language has its own "words," "sentences," and "punctuation." Attempting to understand somebody's body language through one specific gesture is like attempting to understand an entire paragraph from just a single word. You have to read each individual gesture as its own word and put them together to create sentences so that you can understand the language that someone's body is giving off. A common rule of thumb for this is the idea that someone needs at least three words to be able to create a proper sentence. As for body language, this means that you have to be able to compare at least three gestures that a person is giving off before you can begin to understand their innermost feelings and thoughts.

3. Searching for Consistency

This is especially important when trying to decide if somebody may be lying to you or not. Consistency is key in being able to tell if somebody is telling the truth. You have to consider the words that are coming out of their mouth in relation to what their body language is showing you. If an individual's words and body language are in conflict in a given moment, it is often best to ignore what is being said and focus instead on body language exclusively. Inconsistency between body language and vocal words is a strong sign of lying.

4. Context, Context, Context

Context is incredibly important when attempting to read a person's body language. You have to take into account an individual's environment, in addition to the signals that their body is giving off. There are lots of body symbols that have no meaning whatsoever when an individual is in certain situations. For instance, a person with arms and legs crossed tightly together on a cold winter's day is not necessarily a sign of feeling defensive—they are most likely just cold.

CHAPTER 1

WHY ANALYZE PEOPLE

Have you anytime looked at someone and thought you had them understood just from that look? Is it exact to state that you were right? Or then again would you say you were stirred up about some piece of their character? Despite whether you were right or wrong, you essentially tried getting someone, which is an ability that most of us would love to have. Everything considered, in case you can tell when your chief is feeling incredible, you understand when to demand a raise, right? When you understand your people are feeling awful you know, it is anything but a chance to unveil to them you scratched the vehicle. It is connected to appreciating what understanding people means and how it capacities.

The graph below shows the importance of nonverbal and verbal communication according to a survey conducted at the University of Michigan as of 2018.

What Is Reading People'?

When you look at someone and feel like you can condemn whether they are feeling extraordinary or a horrendous one, paying little heed to whether they are a wonderful individual or a mean one or whatever else using any and all means, you are getting them. At the point when all is said in done, understanding someone means researching them and it does not just should be a speedy look, and knowing something about them without them saying anything in any way shape or form. It is a tendency you get from looking and from viewing the way in which they stand, the way wherein they look around, the way where they move. There some different features that could play into your inclination and cognizance of them, yet the most critical thing is that they did not explicitly uncover to you whatever that thing is.

By and by, various people investigate someone and acknowledge they know something. You mull over inside 'charitable, they look sincere' or 'astonishing, they look upset.' These are instinctual suppositions and thoughts that we have when we see a person. As we speak with them, we may achieve new goals or even as we watch them over the room. Maybe you never banter with that individual, anyway you have examinations and considerations in regards to the kind of person that they rely upon what you have seen of them. You are getting them, and whether you are right or wrong is an assistant point.

For What Reason is Reading People Important?

For what reason would it be a smart thought for you to essentially disturb getting people? Everything considered, there are a couple of special reasons this can be a better than average capacity. In any case, at a most fundamental level, it reveals to you how you should approach someone. If they look neighborly, you might be also prepared to approach with a smile and a very much arranged welcome. If they look down and out, you might undoubtedly approach with a reason rather than basically stopping to make appropriate associate. If a friend looks upset, you may ask them what's going on or what happened. Understanding what they feel like just from a quick look can empower you to imagine whatever is going on essentially like that, and the better you get with the mastery, the better you'll be at talking with people.

In case you do not have the foggiest thought how to

scrutinize people in any way shape or form, you could wrap up interpreting something that they do or an action or an outward appearance mistakenly, and you may start to expect things about a person that is not correct. Maybe you see their face and accept that they are a perturbed person when they're basically furious with a condition. Maybe you think they look threatening, anyway they're basically perplexed with something that is going on around them. By making sense of how to scrutinize better, you'll have the alternative to push your life from numerous perspectives.

Understanding people can empower you to acknowledge who to approach with that unprecedented new idea (and when to approach) and who you ought to stay away from. It in like manner discloses to you how to familiarize something with them, paying little mind to whether from a precise perspective or dynamically fun and creative one. Before you know it, understanding people will be normal to you if you practice it routinely enough. Additionally, what's shockingly better is that you have no doubt been doing it for as long as you can remember and not despite contemplating it. That is in light of the fact that it is something that even kids will give a shot every so often, without acknowledging how huge it is.

Understanding People in Childhood

When you were an adolescent did you ever sit on a seat at the entertainment focus or on your porch and watch people walk around? You apparently did at some point or another, paying little mind to whether it was uniquely for a few minutes. Also, a short time later you look at the overall public and make stories. In the occasion that they're walking a canine, perhaps they're a pooch walker on their way to the entertainment focus. In the occasion that they're passing on an organizer case and walking quickly, they are late to a noteworthy social affair, clearly, that get-together may have been with outcasts in your young character, anyway, you get a general idea. You have successfully deciphered what you see of someone to make a story about them.

As you get progressively prepared, you use those proportional sorts of aptitudes to start understanding people extensively more and to some degree all the more accurately. Your cognizance of outward appearances and position start to develop to some degree more and before you know it you can look at someone and rapidly acknowledge what it is they are feeling at any rate, as a general rule. All things needed are a touch of producing for your childhood capacities and before you understand it you are en route to progressively significant accomplishment in your adult life.

Getting Help Reading People

Understanding people is a noteworthy ability to learn. For a large number of individuals, you probably look at is an 'acknowledge the main decision accessible' circumstance, is not that so? You accept on the off chance that I can scrutinize people, at that point extraordinary, yet if I cannot, well, no harm was done, is that not so? Everything considered, really understanding people energizes you a lot in your life and it causes you to be a prevalent individual as well, which is the reason it is a critical ability to have, paying little respect to whether you have a straightforward appreciation or an undeniably expansive one.

If you do not perceive how to examine people, it is a capacity that you irrefutably can learn. It is something that you can tackle for yourself by fundamentally coming back to those adolescent extensive stretches of making stories for the overall public walking around. And yet it is something that you can develop impressively further if you push yourself. The key is guaranteeing that you do not stop and do not desert the progression you are making. You may be bewildered precisely with the sum you can learn in a short proportion of time in case you move on these capacities, despite starting with people you certainly know.

For the people who are not sure where to start or how to wear down getting people, it is absolutely possible to get capable help with the strategy.

Starting with People You Know

It will, in general, be less complex to start scrutinizing the all-inclusive community you know before continuing forward to untouchables. These are people that you certainly know things about, and when you look at them, you can in all probability watch things that show those qualities. If your nearest friend is excessively bubbly and pleasant to everyone, you can undoubtedly look at them and jump on that trademark. Venture up to the plate and see them, see what it is about them that shows others they are bubbly and all around arranged and a while later quest for those characteristics in different people around you.

It moreover empowers us to move appropriately between our own one of a kind perspective and another. Unusually, social understanding relies upon information that cannot be truly observed at this point ought to be translated from moving toward information and our knowledge into the social world.

Moreover, continuously, confirmation proposes social cognizance incorporates reenactment, copying others' experiences as a way to deal with getting them. A real model here is the manner in which we experience other people's sentiments.

When watching someone's face we will, as a rule, duplicate her outward appearance, smiling when she does, glaring in comprehension. Such mimicry may not be obvious to the nice onlooker, yet minute muscle order can be distinguished in all regards not long in the wake of being exhibited to an energetic verbalization. Surely, even our eyes extend so as to the ones we are looking.

Research is beginning to exhibit this to be the circumstance.

Various people with mind hurt, oftentimes to the frontal folds of the cerebrum, develop excessively poor social aptitudes and social direct regardless of modestly incredible insight.

Basically, people with mental unevenness range issue seem to experience extraordinary difficulty with social information.

From a transformative perspective, it looks good that social discernment may have developed freely to non-social aptitudes.

Individuals are social animals relying upon interest and competition inside get-togethers to persevere. So the ability to see expressive motions and grasp the essentialness of social lead may be a transformative objective, realizing its improvement self-sufficiently of non-social information taking care of aptitudes.

Understanding the Brain

In some progressing work in my exploration office, we have found poor versatility and restriction can interfere with social understanding.

We requested a social event from adults who had persevered through genuine personality harm to finish a direct communication task: depict their "ideal" event resort. They were then drawn nearer to put themselves in the shoes of a substitute kind of event maker, for instance, a family with energetic adolescents.

When they had thought of their ideal inn, the speakers with mind harm could not delineate an event from someone else's perspective. Be that as it may, they did not have this issue when fundamentally gotten some data around two various types of event makers. The issue perhaps rose when self-contemplations were incited first.

Understanding social cognizance and how it might be exasperated in different kinds of mind issue holds remarkable certification for better assessment and remediation of social difficulties. It also assurances to open learning of how our cerebrums are wired to engage us to work in a social world.

More Imitation

Inside the mind itself, "reflect" neuron systems in the premotor cortex of the frontal projection are started when we watch the exercises of others. It creates the impression that we do not just reflect considerations, we furthermore reflect exercises!

Right when sound adults are set in fMRI scanners and got some data about the mental state of someone such as themselves, a comparative region of the prefrontal cortex is impelled as when they think about themselves. This additionally prescribes we appreciate others by reference to ourselves.

Facial mimicry can be blocked after mind harm notwithstanding the way that the reasons are still exploratory. If diversion clarifies social comprehension, there ought to be a type of control of the strategy so we are prepared to isolate between our very own experiences and that of others, and move between these adaptable.

CHAPTER 2

ANALYZING PERSONALITY PEOPLE

Personality analysis is a field that is constantly evolving and varied. There are varying schools of psychological thoughts and theories when it comes to studying an individual's personality. Some of the most popular personality analyzing schools include trait theory, social learning, biological/genetic personality influencer and more.

Personality refers to an individual's distinct characteristics connected to processing thoughts, feelings and emotions that eventually determine their behavior. It involves taking into consideration all the traits a person possess to understand them as an entity. Personality study also includes understanding the inherent differences existing between people where particular characteristics are concerned.

Here are some of the most common personality type classifications.

Type A, B, C and D

Type A personality people are at a bigger risk of contracting heart diseases since they are known to be more aggressive, competitive, ambitious, short-tempered, impatient, impulsive and hyper active. Type A personality theory was introduced in the 50's by Meyer Friedman and Ray Rosenman. These people are more stressed due to their constant need to accomplish a lot. They are always striving to be better than others, which invariably leads to greater anxiety and stress.

Type B people are more reflective, balanced, even-tempered, inventive and less competitive by personality. They experience less stress and anxiety, along with staying unaffected by competition or time constraints. A Type B personality person is moderately ambitious and lives more in the present. They have a steadier and more restrained disposition. Type B folks are social, modest, innovative, gentle mannered, relaxed and low on stress.

Later psychologists came up with other personality types, too, since they found the division into Type A and B more restrictive. They discovered that some people demonstrated a combination of both A and B Type traits. Thus, segregating people into only two distinct personality groups doesn't do justice to the classification. This lead to the creation of even more personality types!

Type C people have a more meticulous eye for detail. They are focused, curious and diplomatic. There tend to put other people's needs before theirs. They are seldom assertive, straightforward and opinionated. This leads to Type C folks developing pent up resentment, frustration, anxiety and depression. There is a propensity to take everything seriously, which makes them reliable and efficient workers.

This personality type also possess high analytic skills, logical thinking powers and intelligence. However, they need to develop the knack of learning to be less diplomatic and more assertive. Type C also needs to develop the ability to relax and let their hair down periodically.

Lastly, Type D personality people are known to hold a more pessimistic view of life. They are socially awkward and withdrawn, and do not enjoy being in the limelight. They are constantly worried about being rejected by people. Type D people are at a greater risk of suffering from mental illnesses such as depression owing to pessimism, pent up frustration and melancholy. Since the Type D personality doesn't share things easily with others, they suffer internally.

Psychoanalytic Theory

This theory is different from the regular personality classification theories in the sense that the analysis is based is not based on the responses of people about their personality, but a more in-depth study of people's personalities by glimpsing into their subconscious or unconscious mind. Since the analysis is based on a study on a person's subconscious mind, errors and instances of misleading the reader are eliminated.

In psychoanalysis, a person's words and actions are known to be disguised manifestations for their underlying subconscious emotions. The founding father of the psychoanalytic theory was Sigmund Freud, who was of the view that all human behavior is primarily driven by primitive instincts, passions, impulse and underlying emotions. He theorized that all human behavior is a direct consequence of the equation between our id, ego and superego.

Through the free association method that includes experiences, memories, dreams and more; Freud analyzed underlying emotions, thoughts and feelings that determine their attitude and behavior. Thus a majority of our behavior can be traced to our early childhood experiences that are still lingering in our subconscious mind, which we may or may not be aware of.

For example, if an individual demonstrates aggressive traits as an adult, it can be pinned down to the violence, harassment or bullying he/she experienced in their early childhood. Similarly, if a child comes from an environment where there were very high expectations from him/her and the parents were seldom happy with his/her accomplishments, he/she may constantly seek validation or acceptance from others. They may fear rejection.

Thus, a person's childhood experiences can help you determine their personality and read them even more effectively according to the psychoanalytic theory. The theory is still extensively used when it comes to helping people cope with depression, anger, stress, panic attacks, aggression, obsessive disorders and much more.

Carl Jung's Personality Classification Theory

Psychologist Carl Jung classified people on the basis on their sociability quotient into introverts and extroverts. Introverts are folks who are primarily inward driven, shy, withdrawn and reticent. They are more focused on their ideas and sensibilities than the external world around them. Introverts are known to be more logical, reflective and sensible by nature. They take time to crawl out of their box, and establish a rapport with others.

On the other hand, extroverts are outgoing, friendly, affable, social and gregarious people who live more in the present than worry about the future. They have a more positive and exuberant disposition, and are more than willing to accept challenges or changes.

After classifying people as introverts and extroverts, Jung received his share of brickbats from psychologists who believed that the classification was too restrictive to categorize every human being on the planet. Experts argued that a majority of people rarely demonstrated extreme introvert or extrovert tendencies. According to them only a majority of people possess extreme introvert or extrovert tendencies. Most people in fact possess a little bit of both, and their behavior differs according to the situation.

For instance, someone like me enjoys going out and spending time with people but I also value some time alone for reflection and contemplation every now and then. This neither makes me a hardcore extrovert or introvert but more of a combination of both – an ambivert.

Social Learning

This theory talks about how people pick up personality or behavioral traits from their immediate environment. It proposes that an individual's behavior is a result of their growing up conditions and environment. We pick up specific patterns and personality traits through our experiences. Social learning psychologists are of the view that all our behavior is learnt through our social experiences.

For example, if a person has been rewarded in a specific manner, he or she learns behavior through positive reinforcement and experiences. For example, someone throwing excessive tantrums may have learned through their experiences that drama gets them attention. Every time they want attention they know throwing tantrums will do the trick. At times, we don't have to experience something to learn behavior. Our mind is conditioned to use complex codes, information, actions, symbols and consequences. A majority of our observations and vicarious experiences drive our behavior, and help us imbibe specific personality traits.

Ernest Kretschmer's Classification

German psychologist Ernest Kretschmer's personality classification theory theorizes that a person's physical characteristics or personality traits determine the likelihood of a person suffering from mental ailments and their personality.

According to this personality classification, people are classified as Athletic, Pyknic, Dysplastic and Asthenic. Pyknic personality types are people who are round, stout and short. They demonstrate more extrovert traits such as gregariousness, friendliness and an outgoing disposition.

The Aesthetic personality types are people who have a

slender and slim appearance. They have a fundamentally introvert personality. These are folks who have strong, ath etic and robust bodies, and demonstrate more aggressive, enthusiastic and energetic characteristics.

Briggs Myers Personality Indicator

There are multiple personality tests that determine an individual's personality type based on a psychological analysis. One of the most widely used personality analysis tests is the Briggs Myers Personality Indicator. It is a comprehensive report that analyzes people's personalities based on how they perceive the world and make decisions.

The Briggs-Myers Personality Indictor was created by Isabel Briggs Myers and Katherine Briggs. It is based on Jung's theory but expounds on it through four primary psychological functions or processes such as sensation, thinking, feeling and intuition.

The MBTI emphasizes on one of the four primary functions dominating over other traits. The personality indicator operates on an assumption that everyone possesses a preference for the manner in which they experience the world around them. These inherent differences emphasize our values, motives, beliefs and interests, and thus determine an overall personality.

There are around 16 distinct personality types based on this psychological personality analysis theory. The Briggs-Myers test comprises several questions, where test respondents reveal their personality through their answers. This test is also widely used in areas such as determining a person's chances of success in a particular role and compatibility in interpersonal relationships.

In Myers Briggs personality theory, a personality type is determined when there is a clear preference for one style over another. Different letters connected with individual preferences helps determine the person's Myers Briggs personality type. For instance, if a person reveals a clear tendency for I, S, T and J, they have the ISTJ personality type.

Extraversion and introversion – The first letter of the Briggs-Myers personality type is related to the direction of one's energy. If a person is externally focused or focused on the external world, they show a preference for extraversion. On the contrary, if the energy is inward directed, the person shows a clear inclination for introversion.

Sensing and Intuition – The second letter is concerned with processing information. If an individual prefers dealing with information, has clarity, can describe what they see etc. then they show a distinct preference for sensing. Intuition, on the other hand, is related to intangible ideas and concepts. Intuition is represented by the letter "N."

Thinking and Feeling – The third letter reflects an individual's decision making personality. People who show an inclination for analytic, logical and detached thinking reveal a tendency for thinking over feeling. Similarly, people who show a preference for feeling are more driven by their values or what they believe in.

CHAPTER 3

BODY LANGUAGES

While information regarding what characteristics a person desires people to see can be readily ascertained from that person's general appearance, information regarding what a person does not necessarily want to convey can be gleaned from that person's body language. This is because people are generally unaware of their bodily reactions to their environment, and people are even less able to control those reactions.

Body language will indicate the inner emotional state and characteristics of a person, such as frustration, fear, nervousness, joy, and honesty. The list can go on and on. These are aspects of a person that cannot usually be seen from their clothing or hairstyle. When a person's general appearance, voice, and/or body language are indicating different things, you should always go with what the person's body language is saying. This is because, again, people are unable to control their involuntary physical reactions.

While body language can reveal the otherwise unseen emotions of a person, it is important to remember that it could simply be indicative of a temporary mental state (i.e., depression), or some kind of physical issue (i.e., an injured leg or back), and may not be probative of any kind of permanent characteristic.

When analyzing a person's body language, as when analyzing anything else, consistency is key. As such, the more information you have about someone's character, the more useful the information gained from analyzing their body language will be to you. This leads us, once again, to the principle that you will need to identify patterns in someone's body language, as well as in their voice and general appearance, in order to draw accurate conclusions.

Practically speaking, body language can be separated into two general categories, those being "open" body language and "closed" body language.

"Open" body language is characterized by someone who is at ease, who directly faces those to with whom they are speaking and who maintain strong eye contact. A person with open body language will also not place their purse, arms, or anything else, in between themselves and the other person.

"Closed" body language can be illustrated by someone who crosses their legs or arms and faces either away from the person to whom they are speaking or be facing off to one side. A person with closed body language would also make sure something is in front of them, thereby forming a barrier between them and the person to whom they are speaking.

Whether someone is exhibiting open or closed body language could tell you something about whether that person is an introvert or extrovert, how comfortable they are in a particular situation, how interested they are in the conversation, how much they like the person to whom they are speaking, and maybe even something about their cultural background.

Interpretation

Body language is tricky because most body positions, postures, and movements can mean many different things or not mean anything at all, depending on the environment. In order to discern what body language signals are significant and which ones are not, you should learn how several basic emotions are generally expressed through various simultaneous movements. In other words, you should try and discern patterns of movements that typically accompany certain emotional states, rather than dragging yourself through the tedious, and often unreliable, practice of committing to memory hundreds of individual physical actions and what the meaning of those actions might be. Common emotions and the body language that typically accompanies them are discussed below.

EMOTIONS

Thoughtful or Focused

The states of either being thoughtful or focused are usually characterized by a person being noticeably devoid of movement. A person's stillness in this instance reveals concentration on either some unspoken string of thought (if thoughtful), or on what the other person is trying to say (if focused). Occasionally, a person who is focused or thoughtful may perform minor movements repetitively, such as tapping a pencil against a table top or twiddling their thumbs. A person who is thoughtful or focused will display this body language unconsciously, and this body language will be present and consistent for extended lengths of time.

Some of the other body language that is indicative of a person being thoughtful or focused includes:

- Holding the head in the hands

- Consistently staring at something

- Consistently maintaining strong eye-contact

- Furrowed brow

- Arms folded with vacant stare

- Looking up

- Laying the chin on fingers or hand

- General absence of movement

- Tilting the head

- Leaning back in the chair

- Scratching the head

Bored

People generally become bored when they do not want to be wherever it is that they are and they do not want to be doing whatever it is that they are doing. When a person is bored and wants to go somewhere else, the body will show signs that it, too, wants to go somewhere else. The tension between wanting to leave and having to stay causes people discomfort. Therefore, people who are bored will generally engage in some physical activity to distract themselves from that discomfort.

Some of the common movements associated with boredom include:

- Eye rolls

- Leaning backwards and forwards in the chair

- Wandering eyes

- Furtive looks at objects such as a watch

- Heavy sighing

- Staring into the distance

- Yawning

- Shifting their weight

- Foot tapping

- Twiddling thumbs

- Finger tapping

- Uncrossing and crossing arms

- Uncrossing and crossing legs

- Scribbling or doodling

- Playing with small objects such as paper clips, pens, coins, etc.

- Pointing the body away from the speaker

- Side to side head movement

- Preening clothes or fingernails

- Stretching

- Trying to do something else

- Holding the chin in the hand and looking around the room

When people are bored, they engage in some kind of physical activity in an attempt to stay attentive. If a bored person does not engage in these physical activities, they may fall asleep. Because of the necessary presence of physical activity, boredom is among the easiest emotional states to spot and among the most difficult to hide.

Some of the signs of boredom are the same or similar to those of someone who is attentive or thoughtful. The key distinction between the two is the absence or presence of movement. Remember that if a person is staring off into space and is completely still, they may be thinking something over. If that same person is staring off into space while fidgeting with something, odds are that person is bored out of their skull.

Angry

An angry person will express that anger by becoming withdrawn, aggressive, or defensive. Anger in the form of aggression is the easiest to spot, being characterized as it is by a flushed face, puffed out chest, a set jaw, tight lips, and a loud and forceful voice. However, many people try not to express their anger so outwardly, or they at least try to control that expression, and will then tend to become withdrawn or defensive.

Some common signs of the three types of anger include:

- Flushed face

- Sarcastic or feigned laughter

- Irritated movement of the arms

- Crossed legs

- Crossed ankles

- Crossed arms

- Finger pointing

- Firm posture

- Phrase repetition

- Lips that are closed tight

- Quick speech

- Quick body movements

- Fixed facial expression or grimace

- Shaking

- Clenched fists

- Set jaw

- General tension

- Quick, shallow, or short breaths

- Hands placed on hips.

- Invasion of personal space

Frustrated

The two forms of frustration are surrender and confrontation. Confrontational frustration is characterized by the person who is under the impression that they can fix whatever it is that is causing the frustration by approaching the problem directly. The signs of confrontational frustration can therefore mirror those that would otherwise indicate anger. The frustration of surrender happens when that irritated person realizes that they cannot fix whatever it is that is irritating them. Surrender frustration is characterized, not by signs indicating anger, but by signs of passive irritation.

Some common signs of frustration of the confrontational variety are:

- Direct and consistent eye contact

- Repetition of certain phrases

- Invasion of personal space

- Should shrugs

- Finger pointing

- Hand gesturing

Signs exhibiting the onset or frustrational surrender include:

- Over-emphasized movement

- Hands to head

- Scowling

- Sighing

- Quick exhalation

- Hands resting on hips

Signs that the frustration of surrender has been reached include:

- Hands thrown in air

- Shoulder shrugging

- Turning away

- Walking away

- Closing the eyes

- Rolling the eyes

- Head shaking

Although confrontational frustration can easily turn into anger, it is important that you not confuse the two and thereby throw off your analysis. It is also important that you do not mistake boredom for surrender type of frustration. While several bored signals mirror those of surrendering out of frustration, people who are bored are not necessary frustrated, just as those who have surrendered to a situation out of frustration are probably not going to be bored.

Depressed

Clinical depression is an animal all its own. Someone suffering from clinical depression may be entirely unable to function, suffer from eating disorders, find concentrating on anything almost impossible, and may disregard their personal hygiene. Clinical depression requires medical treatment. We will not here be describing clinical depression. What we mean here by "depression" is the average type of day-to-day depression that we all have felt at some point in our lives.

Depression affects almost every one of your body's functions, including your body language and voice. Depressed people move and speak differently.

Someone who is depressed will be lethargic and glum. They will be wholly unenthusiastic and tired. Thus, in addition to analyzing someone's body language when searching for signs of depression, remember to pay attention to that person's voice as well (discussed in detail later), as that is another avenue by which depression is sure to manifest itself.

Specific signs of day-to-day depression include:

- Lack of concentration

- Poor memory

- Intentional and slow movement

- Relaxed posture

- Increased appetite

- Decreased appetite

- Slow and quite speech

- Lack of focus

- Eyes downcast

- Isolation

- Diminished capacity to plan in advance

- Lack of attention to personal hygiene

- Lack of attention to personal appearance

Indecisive

Someone who is trying to make a decision between a couple of different options will ordinarily reveal that hesitancy in their body language. People stuck in this position will go back-and-forth in a very real and literal way.

Some signs of indecision include:

- Tipping the head from one side to the other

- Shifting weight back and forth in a chair

- Hands that open and shut

- Hand movements wherein one hand moves, followed by the other

- Looking at one thing, then another, and back again

- Mouth opening and closing without any words being produced.

Nervous

Being nervous, just like being bored, causes discomfort. And, again like boredom, in order to distract themselves from that discomfort, a nervous individual will move their body. Being nervous creates a lot of energy, and a nervous person will need to find something to do with all that extra energy.

Signs that are typical of nervousness include:

- Body tension

- Eyes moving back and forth

- Curling up of the body

- Rocking

- Side to side shifting of weight

- Uncrossing and crossing arms

- Uncrossing and crossing legs

- Tapping hands

- Tapping fingers

- Tapping feet

- Throat clearing

- Lip biting

- Nervous coughing

- Adjustment of, or fidgeting with, hair, jewelry, hands, pens, coins, clothing, fingernails, or any other small object

- Hand squeezing

- Nervous smiling (frequently and rapidly alternating between smiling and not smiling)

- Nervous talking

- Eyes downcast

- Shaking

- Biting finger nails

- Preening cuticles

- Sudden silence

- Upper body rotation from side to side

- Sweating

As you can see, nervousness comes with a great deal of signs, many of which are shared with other emotional states. However, nervous people will generally exhibit more than just one of the signs listed above. Therefore, when analyzing whether someone is nervous or not, look for two or three of these signs to be sure you are not misreading the situation.

Sexual Interest

There are thousands of signs of sexual interest that a person can give. Generally, any behavior that focuses on or emphasizes a person's sexuality could be a clue as to the level of that person's sexual interest.

A very short list of some of the more basic characteristics of behavior that indicates sexual interest includes:

- Slow blinks

- Stares

- Crossing legs (legs crossed towards you would indicate interest, legs crossed away from you would not)

- Uncrossing legs

- Tossing the hair

- Chest thrusted outward

- Hips thrusted outward

- Strutting

- Walking to emphasize curves

- Primping

- Wetting lips

- Winks

- Strong eye contact

- Over-emphasized smile

- Leaning backwards

- Leaning forwards

- Flirtatious smiling

- Close proximity

- Running fingers through hair

- Revealing clothing

- Self-touching (adjusting cuff links, smoothing the skirt, etc.)

- Touching the other (hand on shoulder, patting the hand, hand on knee, etc.

- Using an over-abundance of fragrance or makeup

- Over-dressing

- Deliberately looking the person over ("elevator eyes")

- Intense listening

- Trying to create intimacy, such as by whispering.

- Trying to get the person alone

- Frequently looking at the person

- Exposing the neck (such as by moving the hair)

Resentful

Resentment is usually the end result of jealousy or anger and will generally manifest itself as a cluster of behaviors, the object of which is to distance a person from the object of their resentment.

Signs associated with resentment include:

- Avoiding a person

- Avoiding looking at the person

- Any indication of anger

- Scowling

- Tensing the body

- Crossing arms

- Crossing legs

- Tightly closed or pursed lips

Defensive

Defensiveness is a response to feeling attacked, and will result in the person feeling vulnerable and somewhat awkward. As such, their body language will indicate a desire to circumvent the situation, either verbally or physically.

Many of the indications of a defensive person also apply to a person who is nervous, angry or secretive. Like everything else, the other clues you pick up will point you towards which emotion it actually is.

A defensive person may manifest mannerisms such as:

- Clenched teeth

- Clenched jaw

- Clenched or pursed lips

- Avoiding eye contact

- Body squarely facing person (sign of confrontation)

- Hands resting on hips

- Crossing arms

- Crossing legs

- Crossing ankles

- Abandoning the situation

- Refusal to speak

- Exhaling rapidly

Substance Abuse

Determining whether someone is abusing substances can be extraordinarily difficult because people will try and convince themselves that they are not seeing the signs indicating same, especially if the scrutinized individual is emotionally close to the observer. This is why it is important to stay objective.

Signs of substance abuse include:

- Baggy eyes

- Blood-shot eyes

- Eyes that are only partially open

- Exaggerated behavior (talking too loud, standing too close)

- Very fast speech

- Slurring words

- Rapid and sudden changes in mood

- Shaking

- Flushed face

- Smell

- Lack of personal hygiene

- Isolation

- Skinny legs with an oversized torso (indicative of alcoholism)

- Skinny person with a potbelly (indicative of alcoholism

- Lack of inhibitions

- Considerable inconsistency in behavior from one time to another

- Considerable inconsistency in general appearance from one time to another

How To Use Body Languages To Persuade

The Eyes

Firstly, the eyes. Our eyes operate greatly on their own accord- blinking when they need to and gazing where there is movement. While we can most often control where they look, they will sometimes operate on their own in interactions with others. The eyes will often be the first place to show how the person is feeling.

Our brain and our spinal cord make up the pairing that is known as the central nervous system. This pathway of neurons operates fully automatically- that is to say, with no help from our conscious mind.

The eyes are connected to this nervous system and are the only part of the central nervous system that actually faces the outside of the body. Because of this, the eyes are literally intertwined with what we are thinking and feeling, even more than we notice. The brain and the spinal cord give us life- they are responsible for initiating our movements, our thoughts, and our feelings. "The eyes are the window to the soul" got its origins in this fact of anatomy. That being said, it is very difficult to control the emotions and sentiments that people can see in our eyes as they come directly from the places within us over which we have no control. The eyes, therefore, are the first place to look when it comes to seeing someone's truth.

Eye contact is a big indicator of the intentions of a person. As previously discussed, the amount of eye contact someone is making is an indicator of their level of comfort. If someone is making and holding eye contact for a long period of time without looking away, they appear to be very comfortable to the point of seeming like they may have predetermined intentions.

If someone is avoiding eye contact altogether, they tend to seem very untrustworthy, almost as if they are trying very hard to hide something from you. We have all encountered an uncomfortable amount of eye contact, whether too much or too little, where it made us feel like something was not right. You may have been feeling unease but were unaware as to why.

Feeling someone's eyes staring directly into yours with no end in sight makes for a lot of discomfort while trying to catch someone's eye who is clearly making an effort to avoid yours makes for a very awkward conversation. If someone is making steady eye contact, looking away every now and then and then coming back to meet your eyes once again, they are probably feeling comfortable in the situation or conversation and are quite secure with themselves and their position. This amount of eye contact makes us feel comfortable in the other person's presence and feel that their intentions are pure.

Eye movement is also a type of communication that goes on. The eyes tend to go where the person wants to go. If someone glances at something, chances are they are thinking about it or wishing to go there. For example, if someone glances at a chair in the room, they are probably tired of standing.

If someone glances at the door, they would probably like to leave or may be late for something. If you see someone looking over at another table for the duration of your dinner date, chances are they are wishing they were with someone else.

Think of yourself in this type of situation.

On a date where you feel bored and unenthused, you would probably be searching wildly around the room for an excuse to leave or another person to daydream about. If your date is unaware of what your eye movements are demonstrating, they may keep droning on about the stock market for another hour or two.

While everyone blinks at slightly different rates, you can start to pick up on changes in blinking speed. Watch your partner next time they are sitting across from you and notice how often they blink. Picking up on this will alert you when there is a change in blinking speed. Blinking very often and quickly is said to be an indicator of thinking hard or of stress. What causes your partner to begin blinking quickly? This observation will give you some insight into what causes them stress and mental strain.

Facial Expressions

Subtle movements of the face can be picked up when examining another person closely. These subtle movements are said to happen instinctively when a person has a feeling of intense emotion. They are very difficult to fake as they happen quickly and subtly. These subtle movements can be very telling if we can learn to pick up on them.

The first involuntary facial movement is that of surprise. When genuinely surprised, a human face will drop the jaw, raise the eyebrows and widen the eyes. The second is fear. Fear causes the eyebrows to rise slightly, the upper eyelid to raise and the lips to tense.

The next is disgust, which causes the upper lip to rise and the nose to wrinkle. Anger causes the eyebrows to lower, the lips to come together and the bottom jaw to come forward. Happiness causes the corners of the lips to rise, the cheeks to rise and the outsides of the eyes to wrinkle. This wrinkling of the eyes is indicative of a real smile, as in a fake smile this does not happen.

Sadness involves the outside of the lips to lower, the inside of the eyebrows to raise and the lower lip to come forward. Finally, an intense feeling of hate causes one side of the mouth to raise. These expressions all take place so quickly that they are often missed. If you know what to look for though, you will notice them before they are gone. This will be one of the most accurate ways to analyze a person as they will likely have no idea that this has occurred on their face.

The face has a lot to say when it comes to body language, and with so many small muscles there are a lot of movements that occur unbeknownst to the person being observed. This is a great place to start when it comes to learning to analyze people.

Reading the language of the rest of the body can be better understood wher done from the perspective of looking at an animal. Animals' main priority is always to protect themselves if a fight were to occur. They always have their vital areas covered when they are in a vulnerable position or situation and will open up when they feel safe.

Humans are similar in this way. Our vital areas are all in the middle of our bocy- around our heart and lungs. When we see an animal in a strange setting or around other animals that it may have to fight with it will be positioned in a way where nothing will be able to access its heart, its luncs or its stomach area. Thinking of humans in this way will be a great tool for analyzing them.

Use Powe Poses

Gestures and Facial Expression

You can read so much about someone by looking at their faces. From excitement, surprise, anger, happiness, confusion to sadness, all this is possible when you look at their face. Many people are conflicted because they try to protect another person's feelings. This is why they might say they are happy, but their face says something else.

From the facial expression, you can determine whether you can trust someone or not. In a split second, you can choose whether to trust them or not. If someone is assuring you with a sly grin on their face, it is wise to back off. Confidence and friendliness are often expressed with a light smile and slightly raised eyebrows.

Some people can read your face and tell whether you are intelligent or confident about what you are talking about. A simple question might throw you off your thought pattern and help them get a better perspective of you.

Gestures are direct. The signs associated with gestures

are obvious because some are universal. You can convey different messages from your gestures. They are part of body language that helps you put forward your message without saying something.

In terms of posture, t is always advisable to be assertive. An assertive posture is about confidence. Stand up straight, keep your shoulder and legs aligned, and make sure your weight is evenly distributed on your legs. An assertive posture is about confidence. It shows the person you are communicating with that you are sure of what you are talking about.

There is so much information displayed on your face. Awareness of this might shock you. Whenever you speak to someone, they will listen to your words but, at the same time, try to read your face because of the innocence and genuineness in it. You can mince your words or train as much as you can to present your case in a certain way, but your face will always tell a different story if you are lying.

Besides, by looking at your face, it is easier for someone to feel your emotions, especially if they are keen. While some people have mastered the art and can do it, not everyone can conceal their emotions. All this can be read from your face—your happiness, sadness, dismay, disappointment, elation, and so forth. A keen audience can tell your emotions, regardless of what you say.

Instinctive Cues

Trust your gut. You have heard this so many times. Does it work? It does. In fact, in most cases, you are wrong when you go against your gut. If you have a bad feeling about someone the very moment you meet them, there is a good chance you should trust that feeling and walk away.

Intuition and gut feelings can be accurate and help you get out of a dangerous situation. If you are meeting someone for the first time, you don't know anything about them, and neither do they about you. In your first chance meeting, it is always safe to trust in your gut.

The good thing about trusting your gut is that you don't have to read much into anything. All you need is to be relaxed, listen to what they have to say, and reflect on it. If it doesn't feel right to you, don't force it. Your gut feelings should alert you to monitor other observable cues about someone and use that as a credible way of determining whether they are lying or not.

Personal Vibes

Is it possible to feel a good or bad vibe from someone? It is true. Other than the visual and auditory communication, we can also communicate with people around us by giving off vibes. Vibes are about emotional signaling. The fact that we are social creatures means that naturally we are drawn to socializing and will often feel what someone is feeling by sharing in their vibe even if we are not physically feeling it too.

Take the example of talking to someone who says something that disgusts you. You will feel depressed and might lower your eyebrows or shrink in your seat. If they are keen, this will rub off on them too. Immediately, they realize that something is not right. This is how emotional signaling works. It is a good thing, too, because it allows you to understand each other and communicate faster without having to put up with different constraints in your environment.

In analyzing people, it is wise that you become aware of your environment, and the vibes people give off around you. This way, the vibes, and your gut feeling can always alert you when something is not right. The good thing is that some people are so evil, they give off a negative vibe around them that you cannot miss. Such are the people you need to stay away from.

Once you pick up on the vibe, you can easily trace the communication to other observable features like how their eyes are moving, the tone they use when talking to you, and so forth.

Your Hands

Have you ever watched a politician and how they use their arms and hands? The hand is often swept down in a cutting motion when they want to emphasize what they are saying and comes down emphatically to make each point.

Or have you watched how a comedian will open his arms to his audience with palms up, inviting his audience to share his incredulity at a ridiculous but hilarious occurrence he is describing? Creative people often wave their arms around, especially when they are getting excited about their current topic.

Research has found that babies who use lots of hand gestures at 18 months go on to be more intelligent in later life. We can say all kinds of things with our hands without ever opening our mouths, so we should get on and incorporate them into our lives as soon as possible.

Using our hands and arms comes naturally. Even blind people do it when speaking to other blind people. However, be aware that there are limits. You should not be waving your arms around like a windmill because that just becomes distracting and people cannot concentrate on what you're saying. So, let's get down to business and find out what we should be doing.

HANDS

Counting

Children learn to count using their fingers – and sometimes their toes – but it is often used in normal speech to emphasize what you are saying and helps others to remember. So, for instance, if you order three coffees in a busy café, and hold up three fingers at the same time, the server has a visual record as well as an audio one of how many you ordered.

Just a Tiny Bit

Holding your forefinger and thumb slightly apart indicates that you mean 'just a little'. You might do this to emphasize that you only want a very small amount if someone asks you if you want pepper on your food for instance.

Nothing to Hide

Holding both palms up indicates that you have nothing to hide and you are revealing that there is nothing in your hands. It is also an invitation for someone else or an audience to share something you are saying. This gesture could also be used to ask for compassion from someone else.

Stop Right There!

One palm up, pointing towards the other person(s), might be used to stop someone in their tracks when they are speaking. It might mean that you think that the person is under a misapprehension and it is an indication that you want to take back control in the conversation. It is the same gesture as a traffic cop might use to stop the traffic.

And, what's more......

This is a pointed finger in the direction of the person you are speaking to. But take care with this one because if it's done sharply and with a prodding motion, it can quite easily be perceived to be aggressive.

Whatever

Holding up your hands so that your palms face each other and loosely shaking them indicates that something can be one thing or another. It can represent flexibility and that there is nothing firmly fixed in place.

Making a Distinction

This is when you might raise one hand loosely to represent one point of view and the other hand then comes us as you home in on the other point of view. It's about delineating two points of view.

From Here to Here

Holding your hands facing each other and then moving them in or out can indicate growth or shrinkage.

Growth

Holding one palm facing downwards and then raising it indicates growth or shrinkage if used the other way of course.

And that includes you

This brings someone back to the conversation if you mind detect that their mind is wandering. It might mean, 'And I'm sure that you feel the same?' It gives grounds of commonality so that the person feels more attuned to what you are saying.

And I'm talking from the heart here

Holding both hands towards the chest or the heart means that what you are saying is heartfelt and that it is personally how you feel.

Let's go for it

Making a fist shows that you are about to make a determined effort. Watch the facial expressions when making a fist though because it can also mean that you're edging for a fight.

Let's put all that aside for now

Making a sweeping movement with your hands can indicate that you want to ignore what's gone before and lay out fresh information. Or it could mean that you want to amalgamate all the facts available.

Let's get cracking

This means that someone is eager to get started with something and shows enthusiasm. Alternatively, it could mean an anticipation of gain.

Now I feel confident

The gesture of clasping your own hands over your abdomen or crotch should be used if you want to feel more secure. It's used as a symbolic sign of protection. Watch out for others doing this because the higher that the hands are held, the higher the level of insecurity.

I'm the boss

When hands are clasped behind the back it normally indicates authority. Members of the English royal family often adopt this stance, but it could equally be used by an army sergeant or university lecturer. It shouts out that that person is confident because they are brave enough to expose their front body without feeling the need of protection.

ARMS

I'm trying to restrain myself

When someone is holding on to their arm behind their back, they are holding themselves back. They may find themselves becoming irritated and this is a way of keeping themselves in check against attack be that physical or verbal. It's done behind the back because the person doing it doesn't want to appear negative or aggressive to the other person.

United we Stand

Holding your arms out and then joining them together means that you are encompassing the other person(s) into what you are saying so that it unites you. Your fingers might intertwine to show extra solidarity. If you do this whilst facing someone, you might encircle your arms around them to say that they are part of your inner circle and that you trust them.

I am so bored

We are probably all very familiar with this one and it is represented quite clearly by crossed arms in front of the body. The body assumes a relaxed position because it feels disinterested and is switching off. It can also indicate a level of defensiveness, ostensibly protecting the main organs of the body. Watch out if the person's fists are clenched at the same time though because it can mean aggressiveness.

I'm safe

One arm across the chest with the hand clasping the other arm emulates when we were children and our parents hugged us. It provides us with comfort and reassurance.

I'm Waiting

Standing with your arms out with one hand on either side of your waist would indicate that someone is waiting with a reducing level of patience. Alternatively, it might also mean that someone is ready for the next step.

Of course, there are many more gestures, but this list

provides some of the most common and those that you should bear particular attention to. If you want to keep your thoughts to yourself, you better be sure to sit on your hands at the same time.

In the Western world, when we greet someone formally or perhaps for the first time, it is usual to use the handshake. This can be just as intimate as the French embrace because you are putting your palm into someone else's bare palm and may even pull them into your own personal space. The handshake evolved as a sign of greeting and whilst on the Orient they used a simple bow, in the West the handshake was used, palm meeting palm, to show that they were carrying no weapon and no evil intent. In ancient Rome, the greeting was made by clasping someone higher up on the forearm because they frequently carried daggers hidden near their wrists up their sleeves.

You might be meeting someone for the first time or using it as a greeting an associate or friend. Either way, it should be a firm grip and not last too long. When you shake the person' hand, look them in the eyes and have a slight friendly smile.

It all sounds rather straightforward but even a simple handshake can be adapted to take on many meanings. Some of those meanings have been allocated almost universally so that the initiator of the handshake will adopt a certain type of handshake to impress that assumption on the other person. In other cases, the assumption made about the other person is not necessarily complimentary but may indicate a weak personality, for instance.

There are many types of handshake, even though the action might sound quite straightforward and perfunctory. Outlined are the most common below.

Firm Handshake

This is as described above and would be preferable for new introductions or, indeed, for most situations. It shows no assumption of dominance or control but is about people meeting or greeting on equal terms.

Sweaty Palms

This might indicate a feeling of nervousness. If you're interviewing someone and their palm is damp, take this into consideration. If you come up a salesman with a sweaty palm, he is either desperate for the commission or he might not have that much faith in his product. Be sure to check it out thoroughly before committing. However, you should also be aware the 5% of the population suffer from excessive sweating that they cannot control and which is not a sign of nervousness.

Politician's Handshake

This is when the other person cover's your hand with their other hand so that it is encased between both of theirs. The hand grasping yours is firm. This handshake can be used between friends when it is indicates closeness between the two of you. This might even escalate into a sandwich of four hands if you are especially close or if someone is trying to achieve the illusion of it. Or it might involve the other person grasping your upper arm with their other hand, but this is normally only when a close bond exists between the two people involved.

However, when someone who does not know you very well adopts it, they are trying to emulate that closeness which is normally insincere. Don't be too ready to put your trust in them. A handshake is devised to keep someone in their place and keep a distance between two bodies.

Dead Fish

This is a limp shake and is normally given by someone you might regard as being wishy-washy, a bit of an insubstantial personality with nothing to bring to the table. This type of person is unlikely to be a people person.

Bone Crusher

This is used by someone who wants to assert their dominance in the relationship. They might use it to test the strength of the other person. However, it should be avoided as people who use this type of handshake are normally regarded as bombastic and overbearing.

Lobster Claw

This is when the other person's palm does not touch yours, but they put their fingertips to your palm instead. This shows a level of unwillingness to commit to being open with you and this type of person may have problems building meaningful relationships. They refuse to show too much of themselves and share information. Give them time to build their trust in you and don't try to rush them.

Finger Vice

This is when the other person grips your fingers instead of meeting palm to palm. It is an indication of assumed dominance and they want to keep you in your place and control you. They want to show their superiority over you most likely out of insecurity. Don't show any weakness but if it helps you get what you want you should treat them with respect.

Tea Cup

This is like a normal handshake, but the palms do not touch. It can indicate that the person is hiding something from you or not giving you all the information you should have to make a reasoned decision. If you are doing business with this person, check the facts before signing on the dotted line.

Dominator

This is when the person shakes your hand using a normal grip, but their palm is on top, facing the floor. This would indicate a show of dominance because your hand is on the bottom being forced into submission. If you want to let the other person they are in charge, adopt the stance of submission and the other person will feel a false sense of security in their power.

Queen's Fingertips

This is one that might be used between a woman and a man when the woman offers her hand face down as if she were expecting it to be kissed. It is normally a sign that the person prefers to keep more personal space between themselves and the other person, so she doesn't want the intimacy of a full handshake. It forces the other person to shake the fingers of the person offering their hand in this fashion and may indicate that the person doing so regards themselves as superior.

As can be seen from above, there are many types of handshake and the same person might use different types in different situations. None of them will give you a totally foolproof reading of another person but they are often a good indication of what you might expect as your relationship proceeds.

A handshake might also be used to say goodbye or seal a deal. Notice if the handshake is the same as the one the other person used to greet you. It may be that you've won them round and that initial handshake gave you the information about how to play it and get them to sign the contract.

Your Mouth

The Mouth

Another place to look on the face is the mouth. The mouth's subtle movements often go completely unnoticed by the person themselves. We will examine a smile for instance.

A genuine smile will include a change or movement in all parts of the face, this happens automatically and is not controlled by the person. A fake smile, however, will only involve the movement of the mouth into the desired shape of a smile and not involve the eyes or the upper areas of the face. These two types of smiles can tell a great deal about what a person is thinking.

A real and genuine smile indicates that the person is happy and interested, while a fake smile indicates that the person wants approval or acceptance. Another type of smile is one that includes the movement of only one side of the mouth. This type indicates that the person is feeling unsure or not convinced.

CHAPTER 4

EFFECTIVELY ANALYZING PEOPLE THROUGH THEIR WORDS

Everything that a person does or says reveals something about their personality. Actions, beliefs, and thoughts of people are aligned perfectly with each other in a way that they all reveal the same things concerning an individual. Just as it is said that all methods can lead to Rome, everything a person thinks or does can reveal a lot about their personality makeup and personality. The words that are spoken by a person, even if they appear to carry less weight, tell a great deal about a person's insecurities and desires.

No one doubts that the words we speak or write are a full expression of our inner personalities and thoughts. However, beyond the real content of a language, exclusive insights into the minds of the author are usually hidden in the text's style.

From our acts of dominance to truthfulness, we are revealing to others too much about us. You can quickly know the most important of all the people in the room by listening to the words that they use. Confident and high-status people use very few "I" words. The higher a person's status is in a given situation, the less the "I" words they will use in their conversations.

Each time people feel confident, they tend to focus on the task that they have at hand, and not necessarily on them. "I" is also used less in the weeks that follow a given cultural upheaval. As age kicks on, we tend to use more positive emotional words and even make very fewer references to ourselves. A study has also shown it that the higher social class a person is, the fewer emotional words he will need to use.

According to Pennebaker, style words include auxiliary verbs, prepositions, pronouns, articles, and conjunctions. He also goes ahead to explain the content words, which include regular verbs, nouns, and especially adverbs and adjectives. Here is the main difference between the style words and the content words. The content words are what someone is saying while the style words are how the words are said.

Women tend to use pronouns, social words, negations,

as well as references to the psychological processes as compared to the male. This could be a surprise, but men tend to use more big numbers, prepositions, and articles than women. But despite all that, the way women speak implies that human beings are more open and self-aware to the self-reflection. That is, according to Pennebaker, who also discovered that there are three main ways in which people speak when they are not saying the truth. He also discovered that the health of a person is likely to improve, not with the increased application of the emotion words such as joyful, happy, and sac, but with more use of the cognitive words such as understand, realize and know. Public figures who have the tendency of addressing press briefings tend to use more first-person singular each time they are prone to committing suicide or troubled. When people tell the truth, they are likely to use the pronouns of the first person singular more often than other times. When the levels of testosterone increase in people, they will tend to drop in their use of references to other people that they are talking to.

Another study has also shown it that people who talk about traumatic circumstances or decodes to share some moments of feeling down or painful truth are physically healthier as opposed to those who kept the experiences secret.

I earned another honorary degree.

The word clue in this sentence is "another." It is used to give a notion that the speaker has earned more than one previous honorary degrees. The person wanted to prove to others that he/she has earned at least one honorary degree. It is a smart way of bolstering the self-image of a person. The speaker may require the admiration of others to be able to show his/her self-esteem. Professional observers could exploit this kind of vulnerability by using flattery and comments that can help in enhancing the ego of the speaker.

I have worked so hard to achieve my goal.

The word clue in this sentence is "hard." It suggests that the speaker values goals that appear so hard to achieve. The sentence might also indicate that the goals that the person has made could be more difficult to achieve than the goals that he usually attempts to achieve. The word clue in this sentence also offers other suggestions. It also shows that the speaker can defer gratification or strongly believes that dedication and hard work tend to produce a better result. A job seeker that has the following characteristics stands higher chances of getting a job because the character traits could be attractive to the employers. It is because this is a kind of individual who would accept challenges and have the determination to be able to finish up tasks in a successful way.

I patiently sat through the public lecture forum.

The word clue in this sentence is "patiently'. It can be used in many hypotheses. It could mean that the person could have been bored with the public lecture forum. Perhaps the person was forced to talk on the phone or even use the restroom. No matter the kind of reason, the person has evidently preoccupied with other things apart from the main contents of the public lecture forum. Someore who patiently waits for a break before leaving a forum or a room is someone who obeys the social etiquette and norms.

A person whose phone rings and gets up immediately and leaves the room shows that they do not have strong rigid for the social boundaries. Those who have social barriers stand higher chances of getting job opportunities because they not only respect the authorities but also follow the rules to the later. Employers will analyze the characters of these people by listening to the kind of speeches that they offer.

On the other hand, someone who fails to follow the social conventions would stand a chance of getting a job that needs novel thinking. Someone who has the predisposition to act outside the social norms would make a good spy as opposed to someone who is disposed to follow the social conventions. This is because spies are usually asked to violate the social norms on a routine.

I opted to purchase that model.

The word clue in this sentence is "opted." It shows that the person weighs a few options before deciding to make the final purchase. At times, they could have struggled to some extent before making the final decision to buy what they wanted. The behavior trait showcased here is that this is a person who thinks through making the decision to buy something. The word "opted" can also be used to show that this person is not likely to be impulsive. Someone impulsive would likely use words such as "I just purchased that model'. The word clue in this second sentence is "just" and suggests that the person just purchased the item without giving it much though.

Based on the first-word clue of "opted," the listener can go ahead and develop a hypothesis that the speaker is an introvert. Introverts are the type of people who usually think before they decide. However, they tend to carefully weigh on each of the options that they have before giving their views and decision. Introverts, on the other hand, tend to be more impulsive. The use of the verb "opted" does not identify the speaker as an introvert in a positive manner, but it seeks to offer an indication that the person could be an introvert.

A detailed personality test needs a more definitive psychological assessment. However, an observer is still able to exploit a person if he is aware that the person tends towards the side of introversion and extroversion.

Extroverts are the kind of people who would get their energy from spending time with other people and look for stimulation from their surroundings. They also tend to speak spontaneously without having a second thought and use the trial and error methods more confidently. The introverts, on the other hand, tend to expend the energy that they got when they socially engage and seek some lonely time to perform other errands.

Introverts will usually look for stimulation from within and rarely speak without having a second thought. They carefully weigh the options that they have before making any decision. Before entering into any kind of business negotiations, knowing whether your opponent tends either towards introversion or extroversion can give a very strategic benefit. Salespeople should give their introverted customers to think about the sales proposals that they are presented to them.

The introverts tend to mull in the information that they got before they can come to a final decision. When the introverts are pressed to make impulsive decisions, they might be forced to say "No," even when they meant "Yes." This is because these people are not comfortable when it comes to making any immediate decision. Conversely, the extroverts can be pressed to certain levels to make quick decisions since they are more at ease when it comes to making impulsive decisions. In very rare cases do people show fully introverted features or entirely extroverted features.

The personality traits of a person tend to slide along a given continuum. There are also several people who show both the introverted and extroverted characters at the same time. In addition to that, those who are introverts appear to be comfortable with their environments and will usually showcase behaviors that are related to the extroversion behaviors. Extroverts can also display the introverted features at times.

What I did was the right thing.

The words clue in this sentence is "right." It is used to suggest that the speaker struggled with an ethical, moral, and legal dilemma and managed to overcome some degree of external and internal opposition to make a just and fair decision. According to the behavioral trait that is portrayed in this sentence, it is also very evident that the person has enough strength of character to be able to make the best and right decision even when pressed with several opposing views. The key here is to listen to what they are saying and let their words do the talking.

Open Communication

In most interpersonal interactions, the first few seconds are very vital. Your first impressions have a great impact on the success of future and further verbal communication with another person. When you first meet a person, you create an immediate impression of them; this is based on how they behave, sound, and look, as well as anything else you may have heard about them.

For example, when you meet a person and hear them speak, you create a judgment about their level of understanding and ability and their background. When you hear a foreign accent, for example, you might decide that you require to use simpler language for communication. You might realize that you need to listen more attentively to make sure that you understand what the person is saying.

Effective Verbal Communication

Effective speaking includes three main stages, that is, words that you choose to use, how you utter the words, and how you reinforce the words. All these areas have an impact on the transmission of your message and how the message is received and understood by the target audience.

It will be important for you to wisely and carefully choose the words to use. You will need to use different words in different events; even you are discussing a similar topic.

How you speak will include your pace and tone of voice. The pace and tone of voice communicate a certain message to the audience, for example, about your level of commitment and interest, or whether you are nervous about the audience reaction.

Active Listening

Effective listening is important for effective verbal communication. Ways that you can ensure that you listen more. These include:

- Be prepared to listen. Focus on the person speaking and not how you are going to reply to them

- Keeping an open mind while you avoid being judgmental about the person speaking.

- Always be objective

- Always focus on the objectivity of the message being conveyed

- Avoid distractions.

- Don't stereotype the person who's speaking.

Enhancing Verbal Communication

Techniques and tools that you can make use of to enhance the effectiveness of your verbal communication. These include:

- Clarifying and Reflecting. It is a process involving giving feedback to another person of your understanding of what has been conveyed or said.

Reflecting usually involves paraphrasing the message that has been conveyed to you by the speaker in your own words. All that you need to do is to capture the importance of the feelings and facts expressed, and communicate your understanding back to the speaker.

Reflecting is an important skill because:

- You are demonstrating that you consider the other person's opinions

- The speaker received feedback about how the message has been received

- Shows respect for, and interest in, what the other person has to say

- You can view what you might have understood the message properly

- *Questioning*. This is how broad we get more information from others on particular topics. It's an important way of clarifying aspects that are not clear or test your understanding. Questioning enables you to seek support from other people explicitly.

Questioning is a vital technique because it helps you to draw another person into a conversation or simply to show interest.

Types of Questions

Open question. These types of questions demand further elaboration and discussion. They help to broaden the scope of reply or response. These types of questions often take long to reply but give the other person a broader scope for encouraging and self-expression involvement in the interaction.

Closed question. They seek only two or one-word answer, often simply 'no' or 'yes.' They allow the person asking the questions to be in total control of the interaction.

CHAPTER 6

PERSONALITY AND BIRTH ORDER

Nope, the effect of birth order on personality type is not just pop psychology, BuzzFeed quiz-style talk. It is in fact based on consistent research and scientific principles. Chuck aside the entertainment and stereotypes, and you have a near accurate technique for determining someone's personality. There are plenty of psychological principles behind the amusing stereotypes that determine people's personalities depending on their birth order.

Why Does Birth Order Impact Our Personality?

According to some psychologists, birth order is as crucial as genetics in determining an individual's personality. It boils down to the nature versus nurture personality debate. Research has pointed to the fact that birth order can indeed influence our personality owing to the fact that the way parents relate to every child of theirs (based on his or her order of birth) is different. Children from the same household never assume the same role.

There is always a clear demarcation of roles and equations between the parents and children vary based on their birth order. For instance, if you are the oldest among siblings and assume the role of a caretaking sibling, no one else will fill that role. The others will then pick other roles, says an achiever or provider.

Parents are almost always directed by a different approach at the birth and subsequent upbringing of each child. The firstborn instills a sense of pride and paranoia in parents. If you are a parent, you'll understand how frightened you were at each potential injury of your firstborn. Similarly, the middle born is often bossed over or dominated by the firstborn sibling, who is already sufficiently acquainted with the ways of the world. The older sibling is viewed as wiser, responsible, and competent.

Compared to the firstborn, the other children are less likely to be micro-managed by the parents, thus changing the equation between them slightly. Parents are more exhausted and worn out by the time the later siblings arrive.

They most likely realize that their fears are unfounded

and that the baby doesn't really need to be micromanaged. Thus, parents turn slightly more flexible when it comes to disciplining and attending to later children. Therefore, middle and younger siblings learn to attract attention.

It isn't a biological process where just because you jumped out of your mother's tummy first, you are destined to be a leader. Rather, it is about how the parents treated the child depending on this birth order that leads to the child developing a specific personality.

Since the firstborn is more of an experiment for the parents, there is a greater tendency to be overly obsessed with minute details, thus leading the child to be a perfectionist. On the other hand, the youngest born child is born when the parents have already figured things out.

The youngest child is also competing for attention with older siblings, which makes him more of a people please and less obsessed with the idea of perfection.

The First Born

The firstborn child in a household is often believed to

be ambitious, dominating, and responsible. They are known to be natural leaders and often lead by example. These are the folks people often look up to for guidance and solutions. They operate with a deep sense of responsibility and are goal-driven.

Since firstborn children enjoy undivided attention, at least for some time from their parents, they are naturally used to being in the front or limelight. They feel like there's no competition and that they are born to lead. It can be seen as a byproduct of the attention showered on them in the absence of other siblings.

The firstborn child may connect more effectively with other firstborns than his or her siblings owing to the birth order. Parents often rely on their firstborns to assist with taking care of their younger siblings, which makes them responsible and reliable.

They are more often than not well-behaved, meticulous, caring, and conscientious. This comes from the idea that others rely on them. From childhood, they've been conditioned to believe that others are dependent on them for support and guidance.

It isn't surprising then that they turn out to be high achievers who constantly seek validation and appreciation from others. They also tend to have a dominating personality and are perfectionists by nature. The older siblings assume the role of a mini parent while also being insecure at the prospect of losing the parents' undivided attention.

The Middle Born

The general notion about middle born children is that they have a high sense of fairness and peace.

Middle children are generally understanding, adjusting, co-operative, yet competitive. They are likely to have a close set of friends, who give them the attention they've not got from the family. Middle children often receive the least attention and affection from the parents, which makes them turn outside the house for forging more meaningful relationships.

They are generally late bloomers and find their calling after much deliberation and experimentation. However, middle born people are often at the helm of powerful and authoritative careers that let them use their slick negotiation skills. This helps compensate for all the attention they probably didn't get as children.

The personality traits of a middle child are

diagrammatically opposite to the characteristics of the first and young child. However, they are unique, juxtaposed between siblings and this role makes them expert negotiators. They quickly learn to navigate their way through tricky and awkward situations. This equips them for entrepreneurship and other positions of authority.

Youngest Child

By the time the youngest child is born, the parents are fairly assured of their expertise as caregivers. They are no longer paranoid or hesitation about their skills as parents. This makes them more flexible and lenient towards the youngest child. There isn't a tendency to monitor every move of the child, which makes more independent. Younger siblings generally enjoy more freedom and thus become independent thinkers and decision-makers. The youngest and oldest children have few traits in common because they've both been brought up with a high sense of self-entitlement.

They've both been made to feel special based on their oldest and youngest positions in the household. Younger siblings have always learned to deal with their parents' divided attention. They are fairly adept at handling competition and aren't bogged by feelings of insecurity and jealousy. They operate with a sense of security and often know their place.

Since the parents are more flexible with them, youngest born people often tend to follow their hearts calling. You will find them in more creatively stimulating professions such as stand-up comedians, actors, painters, writers, and dancers.

The youngest born tends to take more risks, have an untamed spirit, and are often exceedingly charming. If someone tells you they are the youngest sibling in the family, they almost always know how to wriggle out any situation by using their charm. Don't forget to overlook the context though when you're analyzing people.

Sweeping judgments don't work very well when it comes to analyzing people. There may be several things to consider such as situation, setting, context, and culture. In your over-enthusiasm to read people, you may end up making incorrect observations by overlooking context.

The Lone Rangers

Yes, I know what you are wondering. What if you happen to be the only child and don't fit into any order of birth? Lone rangers or the "only child" is often more mature and confident. They tend to think beyond their years owing to the fact the lone rangers are almost always surrounded only by adults in the household. In the absence of siblings, much of their interaction is only with grown-ups of the household.

Having spent a lot of alone time, they become more confident, independent, solution-oriented, creative, and resourceful. Lone rangers have a lot in common with firstborn children. They also share the self-entitlement and feeling of specialness that is associated with the youngest siblings.

Is It Always True?

It may not always be true because parents are known to set extremely high expectations for the firstborn. When first born children do not meet their parent's expectations, they can become highly rebellious. There is a rejection of his or her role.

It is true that most middle born children are excellent

peacekeepers and negotiators because they neither have the rights of the oldest sibling nor the special privileges of the youngest sibling. Caught in the middle, they learn to negotiate their way through life and become exceptionally good peacemakers.

They are more emotionally connected to their friends, owing to the fact that they don't receive the desired attention from the family. They tend to become social butterflies who spend more time outside the house.

It is a known fact that parents aren't as stringent or careful about their youngest child since they are fairly experienced in raising children. They have already seen their older children grow with the required trial and error, and are hence more at peace. A majority of the time, parents are more financially independent by the time their youngest child is born. Thus, the overall feeling of contentment, security, and leniency towards them is high.

Sometimes, the youngest children don't fancy being the baby of their household. There is an increased need to be taken more seriously. This drives them to be more serious about their responsibilities.

Always pay close attention to how people refer to their

birth order while speaking about it. Do they appear more positive or negative about their position? This reveals a lot about whether their birth order has been a bane or boon while influencing their personality. Similarly, observe people's body language while they are speaking about their birth order.

Factors Impacting This Structure

Birth order is not a precise science for determining an individual's personality. It is a good practice to try and know more about an individual's siblings if you are trying to read their personality based on birth order. In addition to birth order, there are several other determinants of who a person turns out to be.

The Natural Elements

Genetics is the single most influential determinant of an individual's personality. About 50 percent of who we are is determined by our genetic make-up. A majority of our personality is influenced by natural, in-born factors.

Gender

Other than birth order, gender also influences who we

become or the roles we assume within our household. For instance, if the firstborn is a son, and the second born is a daughter, they will each have their own gender-based identity.

The daughter will not be bogged down by the pressure of living up to the boy's accomplishments and responsibilities. If the second child was a son, he would've probably experienced the pressure of living up to the older man's achievements. However, since it is a girl, the pressures are not as marked since she will have an identity of her own based on her personality.

Communicating With People Based on Their Birth Order

First Born

Firstborns on account of their undivided attention status, at least for some years, tend to be dominating, leading and controlling by nature. There are in fact two categories of firstborns. The first is the rule-abiding, responsible, and the compliant firstborn type who strives to be an example for their siblings.

The second category is aggressive and dominating leaders who know how to get things done owing to their perfectionist ways. Be a good team player, follow the rules, and demonstrate a caring approach towards the former category. Similarly, seek the expertise, and stick to perfect ways of the second type. The leaders enjoy being in control and issuing instructions, so you need to be a good follower while dealing with them. They derive a great sense of importance when people ask for expertise or guidance.

Middle Borns

Middle borns are often known to be rebellious by nature since they do not enjoy the special privileges of the first and last born. They often do not get the attention enjoyed by the firstborn or the special pampering received by the second born.

Showering them with special attention or offering genuine compliments is a great way to get into their good books. They tend to be either outgoing or lonely. Try to win the confidence of the lonely middleborns without pushing them to open up.

Give them their time and space, and you'll do well. Do not rush them into anything. Similarly, if you're negotiating with them, you better be excellent at the game because middleborns can be exceptionally gifted negotiators.

Handle the rebellious with gentle firmness. Be assertive yet polite while communicating them. They are good at compromising in any situation, which is why they also quickly take to peacemakers and solution providers.

Avoid confrontation and deal with them in a more sensitive, and accommodating manner. Learn to be more compromising and adjusting while dealing with them.

They may have issues with assertiveness, confidence, and self-esteem. Keep this mind while interacting with them. Boost their self-esteem while interacting with them, and you'll win brownie points with them.

Last Borns

Last borns on account of being "the baby of the family" generally become less self-reliant and independent compared to their siblings. They can often be unrelenting and stubborn. The best way to deal with them is to shower them with attention and affection. They are happy to take suggestions and advice because they aren't very independent thinkers. Don't try to negotiate with them as when they make up their mind, they are almost always sure.

CHAPTER 7

PERSONALITY TYPES AND PATTERNS

We use the different types of personalities to know the strengths of each person.

Let us look at the different kinds of people that you will come across.

Most people have a general idea of being shy, daring, outgoing, or charismatic. But this is not all when you understand the personality type you get to enjoy many benefits that include:

Knowing Other People's Preferences

Every person has his or her own preferences, and you can judge these by knowing the personality type.

When these people operate within the preferences, you get them to be more effective and efficient. However, operating outside the preferences requires more type and energy.

Knowing if you are within the boundaries can help you

improve efficiency, productivity, and even grow management skills.

Avoid Conflict

Understanding the type of person you depend on the personality type helps you avoid any conflict.

You get to diffuse them way before they come up. If you know that your personality makes you intense whenever a situation arises, you will adjust the behaviour so that you are more receptive to the issue.

When you are usually the one to accept responsibility even when you aren't the one that messed things up, you get o train yourself to become more analytical and take time to evaluate the situation before you handle it.

Helps You Appreciate Diversity

Once you know your personality type, you have the chance to interact with other people and appreciate how diverse they are.

When you are in a work environment, the chances are that at times you will hit a roadblock and end up failing to handle some situations.

When this happens, it is good to have a mind that will take up the issue on your behalf and implement it.

Find the Right Career

The personality type you adopt plays a huge role in the type of job that you are suited to.

It also affects how you handle the job that you are given.

The type of personality you have helps you find the right career that will give you proper job satisfaction. For instance, if you are an extrovert, you will find it hard to work in a position that requires you to work alone.

On the other hand, if you are an introvert, you will find it hard to work in a position that doesn't give you the chance to work alone.

Make Better Decisions

How you make decisions based more on what you see and past experience.

You know that when you take a certain decision, you will either end up with something good or you will lose out.

It also bases on sensing and intuition.

If you decide to make a decision based on sense, then you will engage all your fixe senses to gather information, analyze it then make the right decision.

On the other hand, if you use intuition to make a decision, you will most likely feel the situation before you can make a choice.

The only downside to analyzing issues before you make a decision is that you will tend to analyze the issues longer than necessary, which in turn makes the decision to take longer than expected.

The theory behind having a personality type is that we get born with it, and then we live with it before finally dying with it.

When faced with a situation, we have the chance to apply the personality type the right way spending on the scenario or experiences

The personality types are based on Myers-Briggs theory that was developed by a partnership between a mother and daughter combination.

Let us look at the combination pairs that make the theory applicable in all situations:

Extraversion and Introversion

This is concerned with the way you direct your energy.

If your energy is mostly directed towards dealing with people, situations, and things, then you are an Extravert (E).

On the other hand, if you direct your energy towards your inner world, then you are a perfect example of an introvert (I).

Sensing and Intuition

This looks at the kind of information that you end up processing.

If you are one to look at facts, analyze them, and then come up with a decision from the facts, then you are a sensor (S).

On the other hand, if you are one that makes your decisions without having to analyze facts, then you are intuitive (N)

Thinking and Feeling

This looks at your personality type, depending on your decision-making style.

If you base your decisions on the basis of logic, taking time to analyze and come up with the best approach, then you prefer Thinking (T).

If on the other hand, you prefer to use values, which means you make decisions based on what you see is important, then you are in for Feeling (F)

Judgment and Perception

This is the final pair that you can use to determine your personality type.

If you plan your life in a structured way, then you have a preference for Judging (J).

If on the other hand, you have a preference of going along with the flow, responding to things as they come along, then you are in for Perception (P).

Understanding the Scope and Limitations of Personality Analysis

At this point you may be thinking that if learning personality analysis is so advantageous, why doesn't everyone do it?

It may be difficult for the budding psychoanalyst to believe, but the biggest reason is that most people simply aren't interested in learning this skill, much less putting in the effort to master it. People in general are focused on their own lives and how they can affect change in their immediate surroundings.

By being willing to explore this field of knowledge, you are already well on your way to becoming a master of human psychology and personality analysis and will likely gain a huge leg up advantage in any social situation.

It must be mentioned, however, that this is also a skill that requires time and practice of careful observation of others. This isn't a skill that is going to all fall into place overnight, but with consistent observation of human nature, applied over time, you will find yourself becoming extremely perceptive of people's motivations and have a greater capacity to be able to manipulate and influence others to your advantage.

Luckily, we have compiled in this book some fantastic shortcuts to fasttrack you on your progress to becoming a master of human manipulation.

The other aspect of personality analysis to consider here is that you must be gathering data within a framework that allows to to most efficiently analyze and put to use what you are observing. Without a framework to understand your observations, you will be spending much more time trying to gain a foothold on any observations you have made, no matter how carefully or objectively.

By incorporating a framework in your analysis, you will be able to sift out the data that is most relevant to you and know what line of inquiry to take when dissecting someone's personality. After reading this book and applying what you have learned, you will be well versed in the personality analysis systems which will yield great and useful information.

Let's dive a little deeper into the two main aspects of analyzing people: the analysis framework, and cold reading.

The Analysis Framework

The first aspect of personality analysis is building a framework, or creating the foundation that you will need to be able to interpret data gathered from your observations.

When you look at a group of people, for instance, it can be overwhelming to consider the mass of collective experiences, thoughts, emotions, and behaviours that the group represents.

That's why it is so important to have a framework, a lens through which to understand other people's perspectives. The framework that you will develop will consists of a series of reference points for categorizing behaviours.

This framework will allow you to understand someone's personality intimately - so so that you can understand what they do 99% of the time. Knowing their patterns, and why they act the way they do now, you will be able to predict with a degree of accuracy what they are likely to do in the future. The key is understanding the why's behind their behavior.

By sorting people into various categories, you will begin to understand why they act a certain way, and their perspective will become clear to you.

Habits, tendencies, likes, dislikes...Their predominant desires, motivations, fears and consistent thought patterns will all become easy for you to read and interpret.

Another amazing thing about this type of analysis is

that once you are familiar with your target's personality (ie. have spent some amount of time with them observing their behavior) you can even do much of this analysis even away from the subject in question, without them even knowing about it, and without asking them questions that may be considered impertinent or that may give away your own motivations.

Cold Reading

This brings us to the second tool for personality analysis that we will be discussing in this book: cold reading.

Where the analysis framework is more of a scientific process of understanding social dynamics and theory, cold reading is more about the art of careful observation.

Cold reading is being able to understand what is going on in your target's mind at any given moment.

The skills that are relevant to developing cold reading abilities are:

- General body language analysis including

analyzing eye movements, gestures and voice intonation;

- Lie detection, and comparing & matching verbal and non-verbal cues;

- Understanding your own cognitive biases; and

- Developing your own intuition

That may sound complicated, and as if there is a lot of abilities that you need to put a lot of effort into learning. But after you understand the basics of body language and gain a handle on the information, you will find that all it takes is practice, and a little bit of patience, to become very good at cold reading.

Cold reading is essential to analyzing people effectively because it allows you to gather a very large amount of data on the other person, especially if you strive to maintain objectivity in your interactions.

Someone who is very good at cold reading will be able to pick up on all of the signals that someone is sending, whether they be conscious or unconscious, apply the principles of framework analysis, and be able to read someone like a book within the first few minutes of meeting them.

That is the beauty of cold reading. And you will be able to do just that if you practice these skills as well. Just remember that this ability comes naturally with practice.

Now that we have a handle on what we will be covering in this guide, let's jump into the first part - the analysis frameworks.

Where the outer world is concerned, most people present an outer self that is curated, and reflective of our best qualities. We present ourselves in a way that is accepted by the groups we are in. The outer self is also related to how people cope with the demands of work and life, and may be concerned with practical day to day and materially focused things. If someone is not aware of their outer world, they may be criticized for sharing views that are contrary to popular opinion, or they may not be considerate of others. On the other hand, if one is too focused on their outer world, there may be a disconnect between what they are truly feeling, or their motivations behind their actions.

The inner world, in contrast, is all about what can't be seen from the outside. The inner world relates to feelings, intuition, true emotions, spirituality, desires, fantasies, and inner purpose and motivation. Someone who operates effectively in their inner world will have strong self-awareness as well as an understanding of their own beliefs, values and life purpose.

It is helpful to be aware, therefore, that the persona that someone portrays is not always completely in line with what they are experiencing on the inside.

If we want to become good at analyzing people, it is almost always required to interpret the behaviors and external actions of the persona, to remove the mask that they wear to get to the true thoughts and motivations of the individual.

We will use this concept as we dive further into behavioural analysis in this book. It is always helpful to keep in mind that when someone acts a certain way, it may be a coping or defense mechanism, or a pre-programmed behaviour that is there to hide one's true feelings, mask one's true intentions, or even deflect from criticism. Many of the strategies we will learn are focused on peeling back the onion of someone's psychology and revealing the true intentions that lie beyond the facade of their external behavior.

As we cover analysis systems in later chapters, always keep in mind how the concept of the Inner versus the Outer worlds may be coming into play and influencing the way we are interpreting and analyzing people's behavior.

When engaging in a conversation, we typically don't pay attention to the movements of the lower body. Since our direct line of sight is from the chest up, we often miss the obvious signs of the legs and feet. Certain stances that occur within the legs can signify dominance, sexual attraction, and even anxiety. Let's consider a few common patterns to look for when attempting to analyze someone else.

Crossed Legs

Crossed legs could indicate defensiveness. Perhaps you are sitting in a meeting at work, and your colleague says something totally off-putting. You may find yourself slowly crossing your legs as a subliminal way of showing your disapproval. Defensiveness could be heightened when one hand is positioned on top of the crossed leg. This is almost like a taunting move, signaling combat.

Crossing the ankles or knees are signs of nervousness, anxiety, and fear. This stance is protective in nature, which indicates that someone is attempting to protect themselves from whatever source of fear they are encountering. It could also be a means to control actions during high adrenaline situations.

Pointing and Active Legs

If you are miserable at a party, likely your legs are pointed towards the door as you are ready to leave. Our legs inadvertently point to where our heart wants to go. This can be used to determine interest and attraction. The legs, even when covered, will almost always point in the direction they are interested in.

Legs that bounce continuously could mean two things: boredom and nervousness. When you witness a person continuously bouncing their legs up and down, they may be nervous about something. This bounce is like a protective blanket that distracts their mind from their jitters. In addition, when someone is growing restless and ready to go, they may move their legs rapidly. The bouncing or tapping of the legs can be likened to a compulsion carried out to make the irritation subside.

When both legs point in one direction, it could be a clear indicator of interest for the person. However, when one leg steps back, it could indicate that the person wants distance. They may be uncomfortable with the person, conversation, or situation at hand. This subtle movement could be their way of escaping something distressful.

Messages from the Thighs

The upper portions of the legs usually indicate sexual or suggestive invitations between men and women. In daily activities, men may sit with their thighs opened as a sign of dominance. This outward display of masculinity represents an "alpha male" mentality. With women, closed thighs are a polite sign of femininity. Many young girls are instructed to sit with their legs closed so as not to expose their private areas. This closed manner of sitting is graceful and emanates class. When opened, they express dominance and even a form of female rebellion. Since it is so common for girls to be taught to keep their legs closed, doing the opposite could indicate opposition to societal norms. In addition, it is also extremely flirtatious to sit with the thighs crossed and one sitting higher above the other. This could indicate interest.

The Feet

The feet work very closely with the legs to determine areas of interest. When the toes are pointed at a specific object or direction, this indicates where we want to go. This could be a subtle signal your body sends to your mind about certain situations. The feet are used to make a statement and could also be used as an accent to verbal cues. Stomping, imaginative kicking, or tapping are all means of gaining attention.

When toddlers throw tantrums, it's not only their flailing arms, crying eyes, and yelling demands that occur. Toddlers utilize their legs and feet to create loud noises to further emphasize their anger.

When it comes to interpreting the signs of the legs and feet, direction and movement are the two primary components needed for translation. Although we typically fret from glarcing at the bottom half of a person, simple movements could be a key indicator as to how a person is feeling. It's imperative to understand the beauty of intricate movements in order to fully understand the inner workings of another person.

CHAPTER 8

THE ART OF ANALYZING HUMAN BEHAVIOR.

As suggested, studying people is not reserved for psychiatrists but any other person even though psychiatrists are best positioned to analyze people. Analyzing people requires understanding their verbal and nonverbal cues. When studying people, you should try to remain objective and open to new information. Nearly each one of us has some form of personal biases and stereotypes that blocks our ability to understand another person correctly. When reading an individual, it is crucial to reconcile that information against the profession and cultural demands on the target person. Some environments may force an individual to exhibit particular behavior that is not necessarily part of their real one. For instance, working as a call center agent may force one to sound composed and patient when in real life, the person acts the contrary.

Start by analyzing the body language cues of the

target person you are trying to read. Body language provides the most authoritative emotional and physiological status of an individual. It is difficult to rehearse all forms of body language, and this makes body language critical in understanding a person. Verbal communication can be faked through rehearsal and experience, and this can give misleading stand. When examining body language, analyze the different types of body language as a set. For instance, analyze facial expressions, body posture, pitch, tonal variation, touch and eye contact, as a related but different manifestation of communication and emotional status. For instance, when tired, one is likely to stretch their arms and rest them on the left and right tops of adjacent chairs, sit in a slumped position, stare at the ceiling, and drop their heads. Analyzing only one aspect of body language can mislead one to come up with a conclusion correctly.

Additionally, it would be best if you lent attention to appearance. The first impression counts, but it can also be misleading. In formal contexts, the appearance of an individual is critical to communicate the professionalism of the person and the organizational state of the mind of that individual. For example, an individual with an unbuttoned shirt indicates he hurried or is casual with the audience and the message. Wearing formal attire that is buttoned and tucked in suggests prior preparation and seriousness that the person lends to the occasion. Having unkempt hair may indicate a rebellious mind, and this might be common among African professors in Africa, for instance. In most settings, having unkempt hair suggests that one lacks the discipline to prepare for the formal context or the person is overworked and is busy. Lack of expected grooming may indicate an individual battling with life challenges or feeling uncared for.

It is also important that one should take note of the posture of the person. Posture communicates a lot about the involvement of an individual in a conversation. Having an upright posture suggests eagerness and active participation in what is being communicated. If one cups their face in the arms and lets the face rest on both thighs, then it suggests that one is feeling exhausted or has deviated from the conversation completely. Having crossed arms suggests defensiveness or deep thought. One sitting in a slumped position suggests that he/she is tired and not participating in the ongoing conversation. Leaning on the wall or any object suggests casualness that the person is lending to an ongoing conversation. If at home, sitting with crossed legs suggests that one is completely relaxed. However, the same posture at the workplace suggests that one is feeling tensed and at the same time concentrating.

Furthermore, observe the physical movements in terms of distance and gestures. The distance between you and the target individual is communicating communicates about the level of respect and assurance that the individual perceives. A social distance is the safest bet when communicating, and it suggests high levels of professionalism or respect between the participants. Human beings tend to be territorial as exhibited by the manner that they guard their distance. Any invasion of the personal distance will make the individual defensive and unease with the interaction.

For this reason, when an individual shows discomfort when the distance between communicators is regarded as social or public, then the individual may have other issues bothering him or her. Social and public distances should make one feel fully comfortable.

Allowing a person close enough or into the personal distance suggests that the individual feels secure and familiar with the other person. Through reading, the distance between the communicators will give a hint on the respect, security, and familiarity between the individuals as well the likely profession of the individuals.

Correspondingly, then try to read facial expressions as deep frown lines indicate worry or over-thinking. Facial expressions are among the visible and critical forms of body language and tell more about the true emotional status of an individual. For instance, twitching the mouth suggests that an individual is not listening and is showing disdain to the speaker. A frozen face indicates that the person is shell-shocked, and this can happen when making a presentation of health and diseases or when releasing results of an examination. A smiling face with the smile not being prolonged communicates that one is happy and following the conversation. A prolonged smile suggests sarcasm. If one continually licks, the lips may indicate that one is lying or that one is feeling disconnected from the conversation.

Relatedly, try to create a baseline for what merits as

normal behavior. As you will discover, people have distinct mannerisms that may be misleading to analyze them as part of the communication process. For instance, some individuals will start a conversation by looking down or at the wall before turning to the audience. Mildly, mannerisms are like a ritual that one must activate before they make a delivery. Additionally, each person uniquely expresses the possible spectra of body language. By establishing a baseline of what is normal behavior, one gets to identify and analyze deviations from the standardized normal behavior accurately. Against this understanding, one will not erratically score a speaker that shuffles first if that is part of his behavior when speaking to an audience.

Furthermore, pay attention to inconsistencies between the established baseline that you have created and the individual's gestures and words. Once you have created a baseline, then examine for any deviations from this baseline. For instance, if one speaks in a high-pitched voice that is uncharacteristically of the individual, then the person may be feeling irritated. If one normally walks across the stage when speaking but the individual chooses to speak from a fixed position during the current speech, then the person is exhibiting a deviation that may suggest that the individual is having self-awareness or is feeling unease with the current audience. If an individual speaks fast, but usually the person speaks with a natural flow, then the person is in a hurry or has not prepared for the task.

Correspondingly, view gestures as clusters to elicit a meaning of what the person is communicating or trying to hide. When speaking a person, will express different gestures and dwelling on the current gesture may make you arrive at a misleading conclusion. Instead, one should view the gestures as clusters and interpret what they imply. For instance, if a speaker throws the hands randomly in the air, raises one of their feet, stamps the floor and shakes his or her hands, then all of these could suggest a speaker that is feeling irked and disappointed by the audience or the message. As such, different aspects of body language should be interpreted as a unit rather than in isolation.

Then compare and contrast. For one to fully read the target person, try comparing the body language of the person against the entire group or audience. For instance, if one appears bored and other people appear bored, then you should conclude the tiredness of the person is largely due to the actions of the speaker for speaking longer than necessary. In other terms, the body language of the target person is not isolated. However, if you make a comparison, and it happens that the target person's body language deviated from the rest, then you should profile the actions of the individual accordingly. Making a comparison and contrast helps arrive at a fair judgment of the target person.

By the same measure, try to make the individual react to your intentional communication. Another way of managing to read a person is to initiate communication and watch their reaction. For instance, establishing eye contact and evaluating the reciprocation of the target person can help tell more about their confidence and activeness in participating in the interaction. When an individual ignores your attempts to initiate communication, the person could be concentrating on other things, or the person feels insecure. Initiating communication is critical where it is difficult to profile a person, and one wants to convincingly read the person.

Go further and try to identify the strong voice. A

strong voice suggests the confidence and authority of the speaker. If the speaker lacks a strong voice, then he or she is new to what is being presented or has stage fright. However, having a strong voice that is not natural suggests a spirited attempt to appear in charge and confident. A strong voice should be natural if the individual is feeling composed and confident in what he or she is talking about.

Relatedly, observe how the individual walks. When speaking to a target person, he or she will walk across the stage or make movements around the site where the conversation is happening. From the manner of walking, we can read a lot about the individual. Frequently walking up and down while speaking to an audience may indicate panic or spirited attempt to appear in control. Speaking while walking slowly across the stage from one end to the other end indicates that one is comfortable speaking to the audience. If a member of the audience poses a question, and one walks towards the individual, then it suggests interest in clarifying what the individual is asking.

It might be necessary to scout for personality cues. Fortunately, all people have identifiable personalities, but these can be difficult to read for a person not trained in a psychologist. However, through observation, one will get cues on the personality of the individual. For instance, an outgoing person is likely to show a warm smile and laugh at jokes. A socially warm person is likely to want to make personal connections when speaking, such as mentioning a particular person in the audience. Reserved individuals are likely to use fewer words in their communication and appear scared or frozen on stage when speaking.

Additionally, one should listen to intuition, as it is often valid. Gut feelings are often correct, and when reading a person, you should give credence to your gut feeling about the person. When reading a person and you get a feeling that the person is socially warm, you should entertain this profiling while analyzing the body language of the person. While considering gut feeling, you should classify it under subjective analysis, as it is not based on observable traits and behaviors but an inner feeling.

Expectedly, watch the eye contact. Creating eye contact suggests eagerness and confidence in engaging the audience. Avoiding eye contact suggests stage fright and shyness as well as lack confidence in what one is talking about. A sustained look is a stare, and it is intended to intimidate, or it may suggest absentmindedness of the individual. If one continuously blinks eyes while looking at a target person suggests a flirting behavior. An eye contact that gradually drops to the chest and thigh of the individual suggests a deviation of thoughts from the conversation.

Additionally, pay attention to touch. The way a person shakes hands speaks a lot about their confidence and formality. A firm handshake that is brief indicates confidence and professionalism. A weak handshake that is brief indicates that one is feeling unease. On the other hand, a prolonged handshake, whether weak or strong, suggests that the person is trying to flirt with you, especially if it is between opposite sexes. Touching someone on the head may suggest rudeness and should be avoided.

Finally, listen to the tone of voice and laughter. Laughing may suggest happiness or sarcasm. Americans are good at manifesting sarcastic laughter, and it is attained by varying the tones of the laughter. The tone of the voice tells if the person is feeling confident and authoritative or not. Overall, a tonal variation implies that the individual is speaking naturally and convincingly. A flat tone indicates a lack of self-confidence and unfamiliarity with the conversation or audience and should be avoided.

Distance in Communication

If one is talking to someone, the person violates your personal space, and you allow it, then it signals that you are okay to intimate ideas. Intimate ideas in this context include highly personal issues that one can talk with another person. For instance, if you walk and sit close and in contact with a woman watching television and she approves your behavior, then it is indicative that she is likely to allow you have a personal talk that may be intimate in nature. Such discussion may include your health challenges or mental health and not necessarily sexual issues. For this reason, one should carefully weigh the need to invade the personal distance.

Regarding children, violating personal distance will make them freeze due to feeling uncomfortable. If a teacher sits next to a student or stands next to a student, then the student is likely to feel uneasy and nervous. However, they are instances where the invasion of personal space is allowed and seen as necessary. For instance, during interviews or when being examined by a doctor, invasion of private space by the person with advantage is allowed. The panel during an interview may move or ask you to move closer, which may violate your personal space. A doctor may also stand closer to you, invading your personal space, but this is necessary due to the professional demand of their service.

As such, when one avoids personal distance, and the individual is expected to be within this space, then the individual may be feeling less confident or feeling ashamed. For instance, if a child has done something embarrassing, he or she is likely to sit or stand far from the parent during a conversation. For this reason, it appears that one should feel confident, assured, and appreciated to approach and remain in personal space when needed.

Additionally, staying in personal space during intense emotions may portray one as resilient, understanding, and bold. Think of two lovers or sibling quarreling, but each remains in the established personal space. The message that is being communicated is that the individual is confident that he or she can handle the intense emotions from the other person. For most people, they only allow their lover to stay in their personal distance when feeling upset because they trust that the person can handle the known behavior of the affected person. Since being in personal space places a person within physical striking range, most people will only allow trusted and familiar individuals into their personal space.

Equally important is that invasion of personal space is justified because it is part of professional demands. Think of a new teacher that is trying to help a student solve a mathematical equation. In this aspect, the teacher is a stranger because he or she is new to the school. By sitting or standing close to, the student, the teacher is invading the personal space, but the established norms in this context allow the student not to feel unease. For emphasis, this case is not unique as it aligns with stated expectations that people will welcome known or unfamiliar people in their personal space only if they trust them and, in this case, the student feels safe with any teacher. For this reason, the operationalization of distance in communication is mediated and moderated by established culture.

In most cases, one can start with public distance

before allowing the interaction to happen in personal or social space. For instance, as a student during tournaments, you could have initiated nonverbal communication with the student from the other college before suddenly feeling connected to the individual and allowing him or her to move into personal space as a potential girlfriend or boyfriend. At first, the target person saw you as a stranger but allowed you to make nonverbal communication within the public space. When the person felt the need to connect more with you and have given you the benefit of the doubt, the person allowed you to move through public distance and social distance to enter their personal space.

For instance, a lot can be learned from studying distance and space in communication. Being allowed into the social and personal distances implies that the person trusts that you will not harm them emotionally and physically. For the intimate distance, being allowed into this distance implies that the person trusts you so much and is confident that you can never harm them and that you share a lot. For instance, a mother holding her baby close enough to her signals that the baby is feeling assured of security and protection. When two lovers move, closer until their faces are almost touching suggests trust and confidence that the other person feels safe and protected.

Relatedly, if arguing with your child or lover and the individual moves farther from you physically, then it suggests that the person no longer feels safe with you being within their personal distance. Issues that can cause someone to expand the distance between you and them include the risk of violence from you and emotional issues. If you occasionally act violently, then chances are, your lover or children will expand the personal distance to social distance because this is where they feel safe due to your personality and character. It then appears that your prior behavior will also affect the distance during communication.

Nevertheless, they are other issues that cause individuals to extend the distance of interaction, and these include having a medical condition or having hygiene issues. For instance, if you are sweaty, then chances are that the other person may prefer to extend the distance of communication between you and them. Having oral hygiene issues may also make the other person move far away from you because the smell turns them off. For this reason, interpreting the distance between communicators should also include hygiene and health-related issues that impact this distance.

For instance, some medical conditions can make people maintain some distance from you or be closer to you physically. For instance, some conditions may attract uneasiness, and this includes epilepsy. People with epilepsy get seizures, and this can make people feel unease being closer to them because they inadvertently fall. On the other hand, having hearing issues or sore throat may make people move closer to you physically to facilitate effective communication. However, these are exceptions when analyzing space and distance as forms of nonverbal communication, but they should be taken into account where necessary.

In some cases, it is welcome to invade personal distance merely by circumstances. For instance, when attending a match in a full packed stadium or sitting to watch a movie in a movie theater, one will have his personal invaded due to the sitting arrangements. In this context, one may feel uneasy with this arrangement, but he or she has little control of the situation. While we value and seek to protect personal spaces, some situations make us allowing invasion of this space because it is beyond control.

Activity

1. Mark is talking to his girlfriend, and their noses are almost touching. Comment on what this means. Do you feel that the actions of Mark are appropriate? Why or Why not?

2. The following day, Mark is talking to his girlfriend while standing nine feet away. Comment on what this means.

3. An elderly person asks Mark to assist him in how to shop online using the smartphone. Richard is standing right next to this elderly person. Comment on what this means.

4. On Saturday, Mark argued with his sister. He was visibly angry, but they continued exchanging words while seated on the same sofa set. Comment on this distance and space in communication. Comment on the importance of trust and assurance for people who share this space.

5. Mark met his girlfriend while attending a football match. It all started when Mark threw a hard stare at her at the farthest end of the stand.

When the girl reciprocated the stare, Mark moved closer to her after the game and they walked holding hands. This is an example of allowing someone to transit from public distance to personal distance. Using analysis of distance and space in communication only, why do you think the girl allowed Mark to shorten the distance and welcome him into the personal space?

6. Nicole works as a nurse at the local clinic. When one of the patients asked for a nurse, Nicole moved close enough to the patient and touched his hand to examine it. What is the justification for this distance in this communication?

7. Nicole and her husband quarreled last night, and today they sat eight feet from each other while pretending nothing happened. Using the concept of space and distance only, suggest two reasons for this behavior?

8. As a new mother, Nicole holds her baby closer, making her nose and that of the baby touch while making sounds to the baby. Justify why this distance and space in communication is allowed?

9. Last month while seated on a bench in a public park, a stranger walked and sat right next to Nicole even though the bench had only Nicole. Nicole decided to stand up and walk away. Why do you think Nicole walked away? Use only the concept of distance and space to explain.

Major Components to Connectivity

There exist three critical components that determine a person's ability to connect with others successfully. They are; mindful observation, listening with intent, and useful feedback.

Linking with Other People Through Mindful Observation

What is a mindful remark? Just like most of us, you observe people and your surroundings at all the time, but what happens to other things apart from the stuff you discovered? How to apply what you have discovered to support your screening and adapt your behaviors and objectives? Normally, most people work with incredibly little of what they find to boost their calls. If they ever happen to be over-informed, they might find out what happens in declaring what normally does not sit well with the crowd. As a result, they quit conversing. Many people are essential in the making of extremely few modifications to increase their marketing and sales communications. Instead, they dialogue with a person who is definitely excited to participate.

In most cases, there is lack of monitoring and adjustment of verbal and non-verbal terminologies because many individuals never learned the skills on how to analyze people and they change their communication style to be very accommodating to match a person's personality. Remark forces help people to place what they discover to function and generate a livelier exchange of details.

To improve your remarks expertise, ensure to tackle the job like a pup! You heard that right, just like a pup. Pet dogs exhibit amazing interest in watching expertise. This simply means that dog trainers declare the very best approach to show a pup how to carry out the strategy by enabling them to see another puppy perform it and receive a prize. A dog's remark abilities will be excited that they ought to study better through observation, rather than spoken instructions. Who says that the same procedure is not applicable to humans?

Marsha's puppy is very observant; Hannah knows what she will be doing a time structured schedule in the items as she observes her own activity. For instance, if Marsha draws out her operating shoes or boots, Hannah is aware they will be heading to work. If Marsha holds her hair back into a ponytail, Hannah will suspect they will be going herding and working into the storage units. This means hanging on to a car door because Marsha definitely wears her mane in a ponytail when she and Hannah are herding.

The problem is that when Marsha decides to pull her hair into a ponytail, and she's not taking Hannah herding. Usually, Hannah is sure she's heading out to the herd, and she will commence to scratch and pester Marsha about why the turn was dragged. Hannah is very unremitting in her efforts to get Marsha to carry out what she needs as they might commence in the near future. Therefore, Hannah is sure of her potential in analyzing her owner and knowing that she will be standing at the storage door for almost an hour waiting for Marsha's method. Although Hannah reads all the signals, she failed to understand that the same signal could possess countless definitions.

The moral of the story is to caution you that

sometimes you can have excellent observation skills with this particular person. What you observe and affix a meaning is not a preference of what was expected. You can carry out the same issues; however, you lack the desired tools. Your connection does not get better; neither can your relationship. When this occurs, it implies there are modification issues. Stop supposing that the same analysis will apply to everyone. Make efforts for something leading to acquiring better sales and marketing communications. The crucial aspect to remember is that giving up will get you nowhere.

Sometimes you need to observe a little or a bit longer. Don't just look at the person as they communicate with you; watch their communication cues with others. Watch how others react to them. If the person with whom you are having issues and watching their body language is around the individuals they like, make efforts to pay attention to their tone as they speak with other people with whom they talk to in a pleasant way. Simply observe how various people respond to a person with whom you have problems with. How is their tone? What is their body language expressing? How will the ranking be? For confusing interactions, surface area findings are not necessarily enough.

Be mindful of your goals when observing your subject. What do you want from the relationship? Being aware means you can't always be focusing on all the things going on around others, but you need to choose one or two things to observe for some time until when you have a greater understanding of what they are saying with their gestures or expressions. After knowing what their moves will be on something else, you need to be mindful with the observation means with which you are determined to resolve the situation and improve the communication with that person.

Hearing with Intent

People observe others every moment; they listen to what they say very well. The disadvantage is that you can notice an individual, but if you are tuning in with a particular motive, you will not know what to do with what you have discovered. For example, you can hear an individual speak, but if you are not able to distinguish the person's dialogue level when they are conversing or the quantity in which they speak with a system in the discovery of their personality type, you hear a portion of the subject matter.

When playing with intent, you might have the

tendency of interrupting. This tendency system shows where you are heading to after the difference in communication shows that you have a tendency of speaking more than the person. In fact, you have a tendency to speak a lot; you are attentive to the motive of sense, which implies behind the phrases and between the lines.

Providing an Actual Opinion

There are times when providing effective opinions is a way of mimicking a person's price or quantity of conversation. Sometimes, useful opinions will mean implementing a relaxed open stance to reveal what you like to observe the other person do. There are occasions when useful opinions will mean modifying your personality characteristics so that you can avoid making the other person uncomfortable or angry. If your concept is garbled due to your body vocabulary, gestures, and expressions diverging from your words, you ought to provide clarity to the discussion by giving congruent opinions.

In a program, there are occasions where you avoid creating avenues for people to read your thoughts. Therefore, effective opinions will be those masking the way one experiences. It is not about hiding your thoughts, but handling them. It is not about how effective you or anyone else seem, but how you generally show every sole assumption and sensing. There are situations when you want to bury your thoughts a little bit to ensure devices don't present you or set you in any insecure opportunities. In such a circumstance, powerful remarks do NOT unveil what you never wish another to discover.

Practicing these three major factors for connectivity, and other folks might be linked to you. Nevertheless, they might give more support to your thoughts and ideas. It is an approach to acquiring what you wish without mental outbursts and unreasonable requirements. You can maintain your approach since you are a remarkable communicator. You acquire the support from others since they like you; with this, you can quickly get to them. You can attain achievements in your personal and professional lifestyle because you hook up with others and they with you, this include all the results of the few approaches you have discovered from these web pages. Do you have an apparent tendency? Then you've just used the three critical elements to connectivity: mindful statement, listening with intention, and providing useful opinions.

Word Clues You Need to Know

"I Labored Hard to Accomplish My Dreams"

The clue in this sentence is labored hard, and it shows that the person's dreams were difficult to accomplish. Perhaps it took him longer and harder to accomplish this particular dream as compared to the other goals he has accomplished. When we delve deeper, you will discover that the word clue labored suggests the person holds the belief that dedication and hard work can produce great result.

"I Bagged Another Contract"

The word clue is another, and it reveals that the speaker or writer has won so many contracts and this is just the latest accomplishment. From the above sentence, you can deduce that the speaker wants everyone who cared to listen to know that he won so many awards. He is trying to bolster his self-image by appearing successful. To an astute observer, this person seems self-conscious about what others think. More so, he needs the adulation of others to boost his self-esteem. Others who noticed this character weakness might try to exploit it for their personal gains.

"Jim and I Remained Friends"

The word clue in this sentence is remained. From the sentence, you can deduce that the speaker and Jim have gone through trying times. Perhaps the fabric of their friendship has gone through different difficult situations. They probably weren't supposed to be friends under normal circumstances. The speaker is trying to defend why she remained friend with Jim. The speaker doesn't feel convinced about her choice and, therefore, feels the need to defend her decision.

"I Patiently Sat through the Meeting"

Here, the word clue patiently holds a plethora of hypotheses. For instance, the speaker might be bored with the lecture but felt obligated to sit through it for various reasons. Perhaps the speaker had to use the restroom but felt self-conscious or trapped from standing up to go the restroom. You could also deduce from the statement that she might have had an urgent appointment somewhere else.

Gauging from this statement, we can accurately say the speaker is someone who adheres to social etiquette and norms, irrespective of other pressing needs. Those with no social boundaries would have left the lecture to attend to any other issue that needs their attention. People with social boundaries like the speaker would make good employees since they know how to follow the rules and respect authority.

Conversely, those who leave during the lecture to attend to other pressing needs are perfect candidates for jobs that require out-of-the-box thinking.

"I Decided to Buy That Dress"

The modifier or world clue here is decided. It indicates that the speaker weighed several options before settling for that particular dress. This statement shows us that the speaker is not impulsive. Rather, she weighs her options and takes the most logical step. More so, there's a high chance our speaker is an introvert since introverts tend to weigh their options before taking a step.

It's not a sure analysis, but a hypothesis about the speaker's personality. Conversely, an impulsive person would say, "I just bought that dress." The word clue just represents an impulsive decision.

"I Did the Right Thing"

The word clue, 'right', suggests that the speaker

struggled with a moral or ethical dilemma before arriving at the decision. This verbal statement suggests that the person has a solid strength of character to make the best and just decision in the face of overwhelming opposing views.

CONCLUSION

The body is a fascinating group of systems that work coherently to expose our innermost emotions. From a simple glimpse of the eyes all the way down to the positioning of the toes, the body is honest. Mastering the art of analyzing others begins with a comprehensive understanding of yourself. Even different inflections of the voice can change a sentence in its entirety. In addition, the art of touch can mean the difference between attraction and repulsion. Learning how to analyze others assists with social connection and your ability to understand what others are truly saying. The beauty behind the human connection is that there are universal mannerisms that give off social cues open for interpretation. A simple shrug of the brows paired with a crossing of the arms signals a sign of discontent. A slight lean inward can give you the signal that your date is legitimately into you! These subtle cues are intricate in nature, but the magnitude is revolutionary. By mastering these techniques, you will have this unwavering gift that is easily applicable to your everyday life. You will be able to seek the truth and defend yourself against possible threats. One of the key secrets to mastering the art of analyzing others is keying in on your observation skills. The entire body works in conjunction with the brain to send and expel certain messages that define emotions, often leading to subconscious visual cues that may give away the true thoughts and feelings of a given individual without their even realizing what they are doing. Inside, you will find dozens of different ways to pick up on those cues for fun and profit. By being observant and truly reading the behaviors of others, you will be able to emphasize this gift to meet your needs. We encourage you to implement these practices into your daily life to further analyze yourself and truly be able to read others.

The next step is to practice these tips throughout your daily life! By doing so, you will gain a better understanding of yourself and human behavior as a whole.

www.ingramcontent.com/pod-product-compliance
Lightning Source LLC
Chambersburg PA
CBHW050729030426
42336CB00012B/1473